becoming a

HIGH
PERFORMANCE
mentor

—A Guide to—
Reflection and Action

JAMES B. ROWLEY

CORWIN PRESS
A SAGE Publications Company
Thousand Oaks, California

For information:

Corwin Press
A Sage Publications Company
2455 Teller Road
Thousand Oaks, California 91320
www.corwinpress.com

Sage Publications Ltd.
1 Oliver's Yard
55 City Road
London EC1Y 1SP
United Kingdom

Sage Publications India Pvt. Ltd.
B-42, Panchsheel Enclave
Post Box 4109
New Delhi 110 017 India

Printed in the United States of America

Library of Congress Cataloging-in-Publication Data

Rowley, James B.
Becoming a high-performance mentor: A guide to reflection and action / James B. Rowley.
      p. cm.
Includes bibliographical references and index.
ISBN 1-4129-1766-2 (cloth) — ISBN 1-4129-1767-0 (pbk.)
   1. Mentoring in education. I. Title.
LB1731.4.R687 2006
371.102—dc22

                                            2006002316

This book is printed on acid-free paper.

06   07   08   09   10   10   9   8   7   6   5   4   3   2   1

Acquisitions Editor:	Rachel Livsey
Editorial Assistant:	Phyllis Cappello
Production Editor:	Melanie Birdsall
Typesetter:	C&M Digitals (P) Ltd.
Copyeditor:	Bill Bowers
Indexer:	Ellen Slavitz

Contents

List of Tables and Figures

TABLES

FIGURES

Preface

For decades, schools and school districts in the United States took few meaningful steps to provide systematic support structures and processes to help beginning teachers enter the profession. This was a problem. The solution, which I fully support, has been the effort over the past 20 years to ensure that beginning teachers receive such support, often in the form of formally assigned and trained mentor teachers. Clearly, this is a step in the right direction when compared to the highly informal, hit-or-miss approach of the past, in which some beginners found excellent support, whereas many others found none. The new problem, clearly a better one to have, is essentially the problem of ensuring that beginning teachers are assigned the mentors they deserve. This problem—or challenge if you will—provides the central focus of this book, the specific purpose of which is to engage mentors in a thoughtful analysis of their own practice as mentor teachers, with the hope that such reflective thought will lead to renewed commitment, openness to new mentoring behaviors, and perhaps a new way of conceptualizing the very nature of their work.

This book is the third step in the evolutionary process of my efforts to define and communicate the qualities of the high-performing mentor teacher. The process began with the publication of an article simply titled "The Good Mentor" (Rowley, 1999). In that article, I argued that the good mentor could be defined by six essential characteristics that are grounded in the theoretical and research-based literature. One year later, Corwin Press published *High-Performance Mentoring: A*

Multimedia Program for Training Mentor Teachers (Rowley & Hart, 2000). This training program, which is anchored to those six essential qualities, provides school districts and mentor trainers with a comprehensive training protocol and resource package for preparing mentor teachers. The responses to the initial article and to the training program have been personally gratifying. This book is my response to the many requests I have received for a fuller articulation of the ideas presented in the two earlier works.

WHY YOU MIGHT BE INTERESTED

It is my sincere hope that this book will be helpful to anyone dedicated to ensuring that beginning teachers receive the caring and committed support that they both need and deserve. First and foremost, this is a book for mentor teachers. Whether you are a new mentor in training, or an experienced mentor reflecting on your work with beginning teachers, you should find ideas to guide your future practice or prompt thoughtful self-analysis. Many of the key insights are based on my personal experiences in training and supporting mentor teachers, and in working with beginning teachers in the context of their entry-year programs. This book should also be of interest to individuals responsible for providing leadership for mentor-based, entry-year programs. Lead mentors, mentor trainers, and staff developers should find it to be a helpful resource for thinking about the critical issues that challenge mentor teachers in their important work. Building principals committed to supporting the mentor teachers at work in their buildings should find it a useful tool for helping them to communicate more effectively with both mentors and beginning teachers.

OVERVIEW OF THE CONTENTS

This book consists of eight chapters. Chapter 1, *Introduction*, provides the historical backdrop for my conception of the high-performance mentor, including an explanation of the unique challenges of serving as an assigned mentor in a formal school- or district-based, entry-year program. In addition, it lays the foundation for thinking about mentor performance as occurring on a continuum that ranges from *low-performing* to *high-performing.*

Chapter 2, *Mentoring,* presents four vignettes that help bring the mentor performance continuum to life. Each vignette is based on a different beginning teacher and the experience each had with his or her respective mentor teacher. In addition, mentor teachers are encouraged to employ two analogs to help focus their work. The two analogs presented and discussed are good mentoring as good teaching, and quality mentoring as quality conversation. The chapter also includes a discussion of mentoring as a potential pathway for the personal and professional growth of veteran teachers. Like each of the chapters that follow, Chapter 2 concludes with a collection of questions that are tied to the chapter content and specifically designed to stimulate mentor reflection and action.

Chapter 3, *Committing,* describes the critical role that commitment plays in a mentoring relationship, as well as the diverse factors that can cause mentor and beginning teachers to weaken or lose their commitment to one another. The primary purpose of the chapter is to provide mentor teachers with systematic methods of reflecting on their own commitment to mentoring in the context of a specific relationship with a beginning teacher.

Chapter 4, *Accepting,* discusses how acceptance is foundational to establishing a truly helping relationship. Because one's understanding of another person is related to acceptance, several alternate ways of thinking about first-year teachers are presented and discussed. In addition, mentors are encouraged to develop personal strategies for monitoring and managing their judgments of the beginning teachers they are seeking to help.

Chapter 5, *Communicating,* provides mentor teachers with a conceptual framework for thinking about the developmental nature of mentoring, and how high-performance mentors adjust or adapt their communication behaviors and strategies to meet the needs of their beginning teachers. Mentors gain personal insight into their preferred approaches to mentoring by taking and self-scoring the Mentor Teacher Beliefs Inventory.

Chapter 6, *Coaching*, discusses instructional coaching as one of the basic functions of the high-performance mentor. Obstacles that can impede or derail the coaching process are described, as well as alternate ways of thinking about and carrying out the coaching process. The goal of the chapter is to help mentors become committed coaches as well as caring mentors.

Chapter 7, *Learning*, advances the conception of the mentor teacher as a co-learner and self-actualizing person. In doing so, it provides mentor teachers with specific strategies for modeling their own personal and professional growth in the context of the mentoring relationship. Mentor teachers are encouraged to value and share their personal stories for the benefit of the beginning teachers they are endeavoring to support.

Chapter 8, *Inspiring*, concludes this book with a look at the role that mentor teachers can play in providing beginning teachers with hope and optimism for the future. Mentoring is discussed not only as a vehicle for sharing technical advice and professional guidance, but also as a way of helping a novice teacher to develop a deeper and more satisfying understanding of what it means to live the teaching life.

Acknowledgments

There are many people whose support and assistance have played a key role in bringing the idea of this book to reality. As always, the understanding, patience, and encouragement of my wife Barb provided the foundation of support for my work. In addition, I would like to thank Rachel Livsey of Corwin Press, whose pleasant persistence was largely responsible for securing my commitment to the project. I would also like to thank Colleen Wildenhaus and Lindsey Thaler of the University of Dayton's School of Education and Allied Professions for their valued editorial assistance. Their thoughtful attention to detail was instrumental in preparing the manuscript. I also deeply appreciate the contributions of the following educators, who were kind enough to review the original manuscript. Their affirmations and suggestions were highly valued.

Audrey F. Lakin
Teacher Induction and Mentoring Coordinator
Community Unit School District #300
Carpentersville, IL

Tom Ganser
Director
Office of Field Experiences
University of Wisconsin–Whitewater
Whitewater, WI

Kathryn Harwell Kee
Leadership Coach and Consultant
Past President, National Staff Development Council
Former Assistant Superintendent
Texas Independent School District
Shady Shores, TX

Becky Cooke
Elementary Principal
Mead School District
Mead, WA

Lois Easton
Director of Professional Development
Boulder, CO

In closing, I would like to thank the hundreds of high-performance mentor teachers with whom I have had the pleasure of working over the past 20 years. Their stories played a major role in the writing of this book, and will continue to be powerful sources of insight and understanding as I continue my ongoing study of the mentoring process. Finally, I want to express my appreciation to the beginning teachers who were willing to so candidly share their first-year experiences with me. Their honesty, idealism, and enthusiasm have been refreshing reminders of what drives young people of all ages to pursue a teaching career.

About the Author

James B. Rowley is Professor of Teacher Education and Executive Director of the Institute for Technology-Enhanced Learning at the University of Dayton's School of Education and Allied Professions. He earned his doctorate in Educational Policy and Leadership from The Ohio State University. He also holds a Master's of Environmental Science from Miami University of Ohio, and a Bachelor of Science in Secondary Education from the University of Dayton. Prior to coming to the University of Dayton, he taught high school social studies for 18 years at Centerville High School in Centerville, Ohio.

Rowley is the co-developer of *High-Performance Mentoring* (2000) a multimedia training program for school districts published by Corwin Press and used widely throughout the United States. Over the past 20 years, he has focused his scholarship on the training and support of mentor and beginning teachers. He has served as an entry-year program consultant and mentor teacher trainer for more than 100 school districts. He is also the co-creator of other multimedia training programs, including *Recruiting and Training Successful Substitute Teachers* (1998), *Becoming a Star Urban Teacher* (1995), and *Mentoring the New Teacher* (1994). All the above programs use multimedia case studies to engage teachers in personal reflection and group problem solving.

In addition to the multimedia publications listed above, Dr. Rowley is the author of numerous articles, book chapters, and monographs. He has delivered more than 200 presentations at professional conferences and has lectured throughout the United States and Great Britain. In 1993, and again in 1995, he was the recipient of the National Association of Teacher Educators annual award for Distinguished Research in Teacher Education. In 1985, he was selected as a national semifinalist in NASA's Teacher in Space program and competed for the chance to be the first private citizen in space.

Jim lives in Wilmington, Ohio, with his wife Barb.

To the Memory of
Jim Tule
1938–2003
Courageous leader, trusted mentor, and loyal friend

And to all teachers, known and unknown,
who harbor dreams of good things yet to be,
Not only for themselves
but for those
they teach, coach, and mentor every day

Introduction

*The sweetest path of life leads through the avenues of
learning, and whoever can open up the way for another,
ought to be esteemed a benefactor to mankind.*
—David Hume

In 1999, after a decade of training mentor teachers and
helping school districts establish mentor-based, entry-year
programs, an interesting moment occurred. I was making a
presentation to a group of about 30 new mentor teachers in
a large urban school district. As I recall, we were dealing with
a particular problem that one of the mentors had reported on
an index card to maintain anonymity. The situation involved
a young first-year teacher who had traveled, at the invitation
of her principal, to a conference on the West Coast. The purpose of the trip was to visit a school that had been successful
in implementing direct instruction strategies, an approach in
which the young teacher's district was interested. Apparently,
the principal asked the first-year teacher to assume a position
of informal leadership within the building and to help other
staff members in developing knowledge and skill in direct
instruction techniques. Perhaps predictably, the young teacher
found herself in an awkward position.

Veteran staff members, many of whom were opposed to the new approach, resented her involvement, her trip to the West Coast, and her association with the principal, who was disliked by many of the teachers. Consequently, the mentor found herself in the uncomfortable position of not only having to deal with the concerns of her beginning teacher, but with the complaints of her colleagues as well. One of the main complaints was that the beginning teacher was implementing the new strategies, and the veteran teachers were advising the mentor that this was unfair to the children because the teachers had no intention of using such strategies the following school year. After the group discussed the situation from multiple perspectives and talked about alternative responses, a woman, in apparent frustration, stood up and said, "I am tired of all of this talk and all of these different ideas. Can't you just tell us what the right thing to do is in this situation?" Although I was not sure at the time, I assumed that the question was posed by the mentor involved in the situation we had been discussing. I say this because the exasperation she expressed seemed to go far beyond what might have been caused by being involved in a professional development seminar after a full day of teaching, and on a beautiful, autumn afternoon.

MANY RIGHT WAYS

Driving home that evening, I found myself reflecting on the question the mentor had asked, and on my response. Once the question was on the floor, I remembered looking at the group, who seemed to be waiting for "the" answer. I sensed that a response that started with the words *it depends* was not what they were hoping for, and yet it seemed to me to be *one right place* to begin. Mentoring, like teaching, is a complex enterprise that requires practitioners to be reflective problem solvers who recognize that there are often many right ways to respond to most issues or dilemmas. In almost all cases, the decision that one makes as a mentor or classroom teacher *depends* on one's ability to process multiple sources of information, anticipate possible outcomes, and choose a course of action that seems warranted in the context in which the problem is being presented—and *presented* is the right word. Just as patients with medical problems present themselves to physicians, students with learning and behavioral problems present themselves to classroom teachers. Likewise, beginning teachers present their problems to mentors. What makes things interesting and challenging for mentors is that beginning teachers, like patients and students, are widely different and present their problems in unpredictable and surprising ways. This reality means that to be a good mentor one must be comfortable—and perhaps even enjoy—dealing with surprise. Writing about leadership, DePree (1989) put it this way: " . . . to be a leader is to enjoy the special privileges of complexity, of ambiguity, of diversity" (p. 22). Clearly, the mentor teacher just described was finding no joy in the process of trying to decide what to do in response to what clearly was an ambiguous situation compounded by diverse opinions. It was, however, her personal uncertainty about what actions to take that I believe was the source of her greatest frustration. She was looking to me for an answer. I was afraid that I disappointed her with my "it depends" response.

DEPENDS ON WHAT?

I had barely gotten the words out of my mouth when that fear was realized. "Depends, depends on what?" she asked. Sensing her frustration, I explained that her response might depend on many things, things that perhaps only she and the beginning teacher knew about the situation. They, after all, were the closest to the problem and had the most accurate information. An appropriate mentoring response would be based on that information, and on the needs and interests of the beginning teacher, not on the less informed and politically driven concerns of others. I encouraged her to trust herself and what I sensed was her sincere intention to help her beginning teacher deal with this problem.

A few minutes later the session ended, the teachers left, and I was alone in the room packing my equipment when she returned to offer an apology. "I just wanted to say I am sorry for taking up so much of the group's time. I was upset, and I think I took it out on you. It's just that I want to do a good job, and I don't know if I am." I was struck by this statement for two reasons. First, because I saw it as an honest expression of her commitment to being a good mentor, and second because I so often hear those same words from first-year teachers. My response that fall afternoon was my first articulation of what later would become the *High-Performance Mentoring Framework*, the foundation for a training program by the same name, and now the basis of this book as well.

A FRAMEWORK FOR REFLECTION AND SELF-ASSESSMENT

High-performing mentor teachers regularly reflect on their mentoring efforts and assume responsibility for self-assessment. They realize and accept that ultimately they are responsible for affirming or constructively critiquing their personal efforts to help a beginning teacher. I went on to share my belief that such mentor teachers ask themselves, in one way or another, the following important questions:

- Have I acted in ways that demonstrate that I am *truly committed* to helping the person I am mentoring?
- Have I fully and unconditionally accepted my beginning teacher and endeavored to see her problems through her eyes?
- Have I communicated thoughtfully by adjusting my communication behaviors to meet the individual and developmental needs of the beginning teacher?
- Have I employed coaching strategies that are appropriate for the knowledge or skill the beginning teacher needs or wants to develop?

- Have I been a model of a continuous learner who is open to new avenues of personal and professional growth?
- Have I been present in the life of my beginning teacher in a way that has helped him develop a sense of hope and optimism for the future?

That afternoon, I encouraged a new mentor to begin asking herself these questions, and to believe that if she would reflect on them periodically, she would be on the path to becoming the kind of mentor teacher that I knew she wanted to be. I encouraged her to remember that being able to answer "yes" to all the questions was both a goal and a process. She said she liked the questions, and wished that I would write them down so that she could think more about them. I promised that I would. My response to that request was the creation of the High-Performance Mentoring Framework (see Table 1.1). It is my hope that reading and reflecting on the chapters that follow will help you become personally engaged in the process of becoming a high-performance mentor teacher.

Table 1.1   Qualities of the High-Performance Mentor Teacher

Qualities of the High-Performance Mentor Teacher: Knowledge, Skills, and Values		
Commits to the Roles and Responsibilities of Mentoring	*Accepts the Beginning Teacher as a Developing Person and Professional*	*Reflects on Interpersonal Communications and Decisions*
• Dedicates time to meet with the mentee • Persists in efforts to assist the mentee despite obstacles or setbacks • Maintains congruence between mentoring words and actions • Attends meetings and professional development programs related to mentoring • Models self-reflection and self-assessment as hallmarks of professionalism	• Values acceptance as the foundation of a helping relationship • Understands the differences among beginning teachers from multiple perspectives • Endeavors to see the world through the mentee's eyes • Communicates respect and positive regard for the mentee • Models acceptance of diversity in others	• Reflects on what, where, when, and how to communicate with the mentee • Adjusts communication style to the developmental needs of the mentee • Respects the confidentiality of the mentor-mentee relationship • Self-discloses regarding one's own professional challenges • Models effective helping relationship skills

Serves as an Instructional Coach	Models a Commitment to Personal and Professional Growth	Inspires Hope and Optimism for the Future
• Employs the clinical cycle of instructional support • Values the role of shared experience in the coaching process • Engages the mentee in team planning and team teaching whenever possible • Possesses knowledge of effective teaching practices • Models openness to new ideas and instructional practices	• Lives the life of learner as well as teacher • Engages the mentee as fellow student of teaching and learning • Pursues professional growth related to teaching and mentoring • Advises the mentee on professional growth opportunities • Models fallibility as a quality fundamental to personal and professional growth	• Encourages and praises the mentee • Holds and communicates high expectations for the mentee • Projects a positive disposition toward the teaching profession • Avoids criticism of students, parents, and colleagues • Models personal and professional self-efficacy

SOURCE: Adapted from Rowley & Hart (2000).

2

Mentoring

*There comes that mysterious meeting in life when
someone acknowledges who we are and what we can be,
igniting the circuits of our highest potential.*

—Rusty Berkus

*The unselfish effort to bring cheer to others will be the
beginning of a happier life for ourselves.*

—Helen Keller

*We make a living by what we get; we make a life by
what we give.*

—Winston Churchill

On several occasions during my High-Performance Mentoring Workshops, teachers have raised questions about the title of the program. "Why do you call it high-performance mentoring?" "Aren't all mentors high-performing?" And, "What about the beginning teachers, don't they have to perform as well if the relationship is going to work?" In response to the first question, I explain that I use the term high-performance mentor to imply that there are qualitatively different levels of mentor performance. The answer to the second question is related to the first. No, unfortunately, not all mentors are high-performing. The answer to the third question, regarding the beginning teachers and their role in the mentoring relationship, is not as easy to answer. In Chapter 3, I will more fully explore the role that commitment plays in a mentoring relationship. For now, one important perspective is simply this. High-performance mentors persist in their efforts to help beginning teachers, even when the beginning teacher does not evidence commitment to the relationship. They recognize that building a mutually satisfying relationship does take two, but they also accept that a host of factors can and often do influence beginning teachers to not fully commit to the mentoring process.

Low- to High-Performance Mentoring

The performance of mentor teachers working in school-based programs can, and often does, vary across a continuum that ranges from very low to very high. This fact, as disconcerting as it might be, should come as no surprise, for a couple of important reasons. First, human relationships are complex and flourish or fail in diverse contexts of time and space. And this is true even in relationships where both people chose to enter the relationship, which is often not the case in school-based mentoring programs. If any two people endeavoring to build or maintain a relationship fail to find the time and the space to meet and have honest and respectful dialogue, the relationship is likely to be arrested at a relatively low level, or may fail completely. Second, the complexities and competing demands of life and living work against people finding the time and space to build meaningful relationships. These basic facts apply broadly to virtually all human relationships, with obvious implications for the mentoring of beginning teachers.

Mentoring a beginning teacher can be a challenging, rewarding, and mutually satisfying experience that contributes to the personal and professional growth of both the mentor and the novice teacher. This I know to be true. However, this I also know to be true: Mentoring a beginning teacher can be an effortless, disappointing, and mutually unsatisfying experience that contributes little or nothing to the personal or professional growth of the mentor or the novice teacher. I realize that this is perhaps an odd way to begin a book on becoming a high-performance mentor teacher, yet there is an important point to be made. Mentoring in today's elementary and secondary school environments is a unique enterprise that occurs in diverse contexts with often unpredictable and uneven effects. The problem, stated in a different way, is that a *mentor teacher* might not actually be a mentor. And conversely, a teacher who is not *the mentor teacher* might be the mentor. If you are a classroom teacher or building principal who is even a casual observer of school life, you know what I am talking about.

When working with beginning teachers, as I often do in my role as a university-based teacher educator, I frequently find the opportunity to talk with them about their first year of teaching and their mentoring relationships. I typically begin with a simple probe such as "So, how is it going so far?" When I receive the somewhat predictable "just fine" or "it's going great" I follow with a new prompt. "Okay, now that we have that out of the way, how is it *really* going?" This probe often uncovers a more honest rendering of the struggles that are predictably associated with the first year of practice. As specific problems are revealed, I take the opportunity to ask beginning teachers if their mentors have been helpful in dealing with those problems. I ask this question with no interest in evaluating the performance of individual mentors, but rather to gain insight into how beginning teachers vary in their perceptions of their mentoring relationships. I fully understand that in asking beginning teachers for such perspectives I am not getting the full picture. Certainly, I am not coming at the story from the other important perspective, that of the mentor teacher. Nonetheless, such conversations have consistently reinforced my earlier claim that mentoring relationships vary widely in quality. Consider, for example, the following answers from four beginning teachers.

"Mentor? What mentor? I haven't met mine yet." By the way, it was mid-November when that conversation took place. Here is another answer I encounter far too often: "I am not sure how it's going. We haven't talked for a while." Or, consider this response. "Not that great. We got off to a rough start and it has been downhill from there." Now, before you get discouraged, I frequently receive testimonials similar to the following: "It's been wonderful. She is very accessible and yet gives me space as well. I can't imagine getting through this year without her help." The point of sharing such beginning teacher perspectives is not to suggest that only one in four mentoring relationships is successful, but rather to make clear that the quality of such relationships varies widely. The quality of any relationship is largely a function of the commitment that both people have to making the relationship work. Keeping in mind the idea that *it takes two,* let's take a deeper look at what lay beneath the four beginning teacher comments.

What Mentor?

Colleen was a first-year, third-grade teacher working in a large elementary school in a suburban school district with a newly established entry-year program. Colleen's mentor, Janice, was in her 27th year of teaching fifth grade. Janice received a phone call from her principal late one August afternoon. "We have a new third-grade teacher and I have to give her a mentor," the principal explained. "I just wanted to let you know that I sent your name over to the board office. I hope that's okay. I know you'll do a great job." Caught off guard by the call, Janice agreed to the assignment. Thinking about it later that evening, she told her husband that she was having second thoughts. "I'm not sure I'm the right person to be anybody's mentor right now. I'm having enough trouble getting through the school year with all of the new stuff they keep piling on." As the school year began, Janice became quickly immersed in her own classroom challenges and failed to introduce herself to Colleen. After a couple of weeks passed, Janice began feeling guilty about not introducing herself and offering help. Colleen, on the other hand, was not sure what to do. She had connected with Sharon, a veteran teacher on her third-grade team, and was getting lots of great ideas and encouragement as well. Colleen had wondered from the beginning how a fifth-grade teacher could help with her third-grade curriculum, so she was happy to have Sharon's support. With each passing week, it became increasingly uncomfortable for Janice to think about how to start a relationship with Colleen. She frequently observed Colleen talking and laughing with Sharon and eventually concluded that Colleen didn't need her help. Meanwhile, the mentor-mentee list filed at the board office recorded Colleen's and Janice's names, side-by-side.

We Haven't Talked for a While

It was April when I had a chance to sit down and talk with Tony about his first-year experience in teaching geometry and Algebra I in a mid-sized urban high school. After listening to Tony describe his first year of teaching as "a real learning experience," I asked what role his mentor, Steve, had played in that learning. "None, really," he said. "We talked at the beginning of the school year and he helped me find some stuff I needed for my room, but that's been about it." "That's it?" I asked. "Yeah, pretty much. I mean, we pass each other in the hall and he always asks how it's going. I usually just say 'fine' or give him a thumbs-up sign. When we met in August he told me what room he was in and said I should feel free to come down whenever I needed help." "And you haven't taken him up on that offer?" I queried. "Not really, he's really busy with coaching on top of teaching, and I don't want to be a burden. Plus, I kind of like having to figure things out on my own." From Steve's perspective, he had helped Tony get off on the right foot by making sure he had enough desks in his class-room and by helping him grab a better overhead projector from the classroom of a recently retired colleague. He also felt good about his sincere offer to provide additional help. Fortunately, things seemed to be going pretty well because Tony hadn't been down to see him.

Off to a Bad Start

According to a beginning teacher named Angie, it was the day before school started when she first met Carmen, her assigned mentor. Angie had just finished decorating her classroom in preparation for welcoming her sixth-grade science students the following day. Angie had hung colorful posters around the room. Some featured inspirational quotes below dramatic pictures of men and women engaged in challenging outdoor activities, such as mountain climbing and whitewater kayaking. Other posters featured famous athletes and singers popular with middle school students. From Angie's perspective, the room looked warm, inviting, and fun. "It was just the kind of atmosphere I always dreamed about creating once I had my own classroom," she explained. Unfortunately, that perspective was not shared by Carmen. After entering the classroom and introducing herself as Angie's mentor, Carmen began examining the room with a concerned look on her face. "You need to get this classroom ready for science instruction. These posters have nothing to do with science or scientists. You need to create a more academic climate or these kids are going to run you out of town." Angie was hurt and struggled to disguise her emotions as Carmen proceeded to inspect the room while asking questions about what Angie planned to do on the first day of school. When Angie described an interest inventory she planned to have her students complete, Carmen suggested Angie start instead with explaining her discipline policy. "Lay the law down early and make it stick if you want to make it in this world." By the time Carmen left the room, Angie was on the verge of tears. When she was gone, the tears came. Carmen, in contrast, drove home feeling good about the sound advice she had provided. She sensed that Angie was not happy with all the suggestions she gave, but was totally confident she would thank her later.

It's Been Wonderful

In contrast to the above scenarios, a first-year teacher named Judy could not have been more positive about the relationship she had with her mentor. "To be honest, I had some early reservations about having a mentor," Judy began. Having just finished student teaching, I guess I was anxious to be on my own, to have my own room, my own students. I don't know, I guess I just didn't know what to expect from a mentor. Now, I can't imagine what this year would be like without Beth." Beth, a 10-year veteran teacher and experienced mentor, was assigned to work with Judy by the district's mentoring committee, which matched the two based on Judy's job as an intervention specialist and Beth's prior experience as a special education teacher. Beth was currently teaching fourth grade in the same building where Judy had responsibility for servicing students in Grades 1 through 5. Their relationship had gotten off to a good start when Beth gave Judy a call in early August inviting her to a cookout at her house. Judy enjoyed meeting Beth's husband, Jack, and their two young children. After dinner, Jack and the kids left for the mall to see a movie. Beth and Judy sat on the patio and talked into the evening. Driving home to her new apartment later that night, Judy felt a mix of relief and excitement. She was relieved to know that Beth seemed genuinely interested in her success and very respectful of her ideas as well. She was excited because she had truly enjoyed the evening and was looking forward to perhaps having a new friend. Later that same night when Jack returned home, he asked Beth how things went. "It went great. Thanks for taking the kids to the movie. I think we are off to a good start. She is going to be a real asset to our building. She has a tough road ahead, though—I just hope I can help her deal with the potholes." "You know you will. She's lucky to have you," was Jack's reply.

The first three vignettes serve as examples of three basic ways by which a mentor teacher can fail to become a high-performance mentor, the first of which is failing to show up for the job.

Failing to Show Up for the Job

The first way a mentor teacher can fail is to simply not show up for the job. Such individuals typically lack any real commitment to supporting the beginning teacher to whom they have been assigned. In many cases, this phenomenon occurs in school districts with very informal entry-year support programs, or in specific buildings where the school culture places little value on mentoring. It has always intrigued me why a veteran teacher would agree to support a beginning teacher, agree to be a mentor, and then abandon the responsibilities associated with that role. There are of course many factors that might influence this behavior, and these will be discussed in Chapter 3 in an exploration of the role of commitment in high-performance mentoring. In the opening vignette titled "What Mentor?" you will remember that the first-year teacher, Colleen, never met her *formal* mentor Janice, but found support and guidance from her grade-level colleague, Sharon. In the end, it appeared that Janice used this observation to rationalize her decision not to begin the mentoring process. As a cautionary note, I would not want readers to conclude that the real problem in this scenario was the lack of a grade-level match. While teaching the same grade level may have been a factor that helped Colleen and Sharon build rapport, the lack of grade-level match was not instrumental in Janice's failure to commit. Other forces in Janice's personal and professional life seemed to be at work.

Not Staying on the Job

The second way in which veteran teachers can fail to meet the standard of high-performance mentoring is by failing to take the initiatives to build a relationship over time. This phenomenon occurs more frequently than the first problem of not showing up for the job. Many mentor teachers start with good intentions and a vision of how they hope the mentoring relationship will develop, but subsequently fail to take the steps necessary to realize that vision. In contrast, still others start with a very limited conception of their role and the impact they might have on the life of a beginning teacher. Such limited conceptions often become self-fulfilling prophecies. Such was the case in the vignette titled "We Haven't Talked for a While." Steve, the mentor in this case, seemed to have a rather narrow conception of his responsibilities as a mentor, perhaps believing that it was up to Tony, the beginning teacher, to assume responsibility for seeking help. When Tony didn't take that initiative, Steve concluded that everything was going well. Of course, a first year of teaching in which everything goes well is hardly the norm. By the way, this is not to imply that all blame for the failed relationship rests on Steve. As in the first vignette, the beginning teacher contributed to the problem. In this case, Tony liked the autonomy that Steve afforded him because he felt it gave him room to experiment and learn things on his own. The potential problem in this situation was that Steve's decision to take a laissez-faire approach did not seem to be based on any careful considera-tion of Tony's needs, but rather on Steve's personal belief that it was Tony's responsibility to seek help.

Showing Up, Staying On, and Failing Anyway

In the case of "Off to a Bad Start" you were introduced to a mentor teacher named Carmen and her strongly held beli-efs about what constitute effective middle school prac-tices. Carmen took her mentor assignment quite seriously and stayed committed to the job throughout the school year. The only problem was that Angie hoped and prayed that she would leave her alone. In each of their meetings, Carmen made it clear that Angie would be a success if she would just follow her advice. Carmen rarely if ever asked Angie for her thoughts on a classroom issue or situation. And when she did, the question usually began with an accusatory "why." Why Carmen felt such a strong need to control Angie's develop-ment is an interesting question for which I have no answer. The only thing I know for sure is that it did not seem to be based on a real consideration of Angie's classroom perfor-mances or professional commitment. My guess is that her controlling approach was meeting some personal need rather than any respect for needs that Angie may have had. Quite to the contrary, Angie, like many beginning teachers, had a strong need to be accepted into the school community and to be respected by her colleagues. She also had an understandable need to express herself and her ideas in the classroom. Unfortunately, Carmen met none of these basic needs and only increased Angie's anxiety and doubt.

QUALITY MENTORING AS QUALITY CONVERSATION

Clearly there are many ways to conceptualize a mentoring relationship. Typically, however, such conceptions tend to focus on the role of the mentor. For example, conceptions such as coach, counselor, political advisor, role model, guide, or resource person all tend to focus on images of the mentor at work. Such images are important and each is worthy of analysis in terms of its implications for mentoring. In addition, when considered collectively, they present a multifaceted portrait of the diverse roles that mentors play in supporting beginning teachers. Recently, however, I have been particularly drawn to a simile for mentoring that captures, from my perspective, the very heart of the process. Consider, if you will, the conception of mentoring as a *good conversation.*

Reflecting back on our vignettes, each could be analyzed from this perspective. In the case of "What Mentor?" there was no conversation because Janice never introduced herself, never initiated the dialogue. In the case of "We Haven't Talked for a While," the conversation got off to a good start when Steve talked with Tony and helped him find resources for his room. Unfortunately, the conversation died quickly as Steve waited for Tony to reengage him, which he never did. Then of course you remember Carmen, the mentor in "Off to a Bad Start." In this case, there was a lot of talk going on, but it failed to meet the test of good conversation, as Angie had little opportunity to share her perspectives and over time came to view Carmen as a toxic force in her life. Finally, in "It's Been Wonderful," we have an image of two people finding the time and space to have a meaningful and respectful conversation that left both mentor and mentee looking forward to the next opportunity to continue the dialogue.

Several years ago, Brother Raymond Fitz, then President of the University of Dayton, made a speech to the faculty that I found particularly memorable. In that speech, he spoke of the idea of the university as a *conversation*. By this he meant that, at its best, a university is defined by the quality of dialogue between and among professors and students in common pursuit of the answers to life's most compelling questions and humankind's most troubling problems. Similarly, the quality of a mentoring relationship can only be as good as the quality of the conversation that connects the mentor and the beginning teacher. If the conversation is superficial and focused on the trivial, so likely will be the relationship. If, by contrast, the conversation is deep and focused on the meaningful, so likely will be the relationship. A mentoring relationship, at its best, finds mentors and beginning teachers in common pursuit of answers to our profession's most compelling questions and solutions to its most troubling problems. These, of course, are the questions and problems that inevitably focus on student learning and what we as teachers can do to motivate and support that learning. Perhaps the most significant challenge for any mentor teacher is to help beginning teachers join that conversation, which hopefully will sustain and inspire them throughout their teaching lives.

GOOD MENTORING AS GOOD TEACHING

High-performing mentors understand that, in many ways, being the good mentor is not unlike being the good teacher. Both proceed in their daily actions with a heartfelt belief that they can be helpful, that they can make a difference in the life of another. At the same time, they do so with deep understanding of the reality that individuals are ultimately responsible for making changes in their own lives. The most caring mentor cannot help the struggling, beginning teacher who is not ready for change, and not open to the help of another. In the same way, no dedicated teacher can help the struggling student find success in mastering new or difficult material if that student is not at least open to being taught. In other words, the ancient notion that "when the student is ready, the teacher will appear," holds true. With this knowledge, being the good mentor, being the good teacher, becomes an even nobler enterprise as both continue to take action believing that with caring tenacity they will eventually make the break-through that will lead to the ultimate success of the one they seek to help. In other words, both practice what might be best described as acts of applied faith. High-performance mentors have and keep the faith, and do so even when the beginning teachers they are trying to help are less responsive or more defensive than they would like. Mentor teachers operating at lower levels have little tolerance for such behaviors and quickly use them as excuses for lowering the expectations they held for their own performance and for the growth of the beginning teacher.

Another important way in which mentoring and teaching are alike involves the need to respond thoughtfully to the dif-ferences in the groups of students one teaches, or to the differ-ences in the beginning teachers one seeks to mentor. Teachers are quick to acknowledge that each new school year is inter-esting and challenging, in part because they can never accu-rately predict what type of class or classes they will encounter. The character, dynamic, or personality of different classes varies widely from year to year. Each year, consequently, pre-sents new challenges and opportunities. In similar fashion, veteran mentors understand how each mentoring experience is profoundly affected by the differences they encounter in the beginning teachers they seek to support. Because of this reality, it is difficult, in many respects, to know what kind of teacher or mentor you might need to be in advance of meeting and getting to know the students you will teach, or the new teacher you will mentor. Chapter 4, which focuses on the role of acceptance in a mentoring relationship, will explore multi-ple frameworks for thinking about the many and varied ways in which beginning teachers are different.

Just as teachers and students in a classroom setting develop different relationships, mentor and beginning teachers develop different relationships as well. One year a mentoring relationship may evolve into a significant friendship. The next year the same mentor might describe the relationship with a new mentee as more professional in nature. It's important to remember that there are many types of relationships that can be helpful to beginning teachers, and mentors consequently need not feel the pressure or necessity of finding a new and perhaps life-long friend. Nonetheless, friendship can be an unexpected gift of the mentoring experience. In contrast, other mentoring relationships provide the gift of a new and respected colleague. And still others require extraordinary efforts on the part of the mentor just to open and maintain the most basic lines of communication.

One thing I have learned is that the relationships between mentors and mentees are complex, idiosyncratic, and very much a function of the personal biographies, needs, interests, and dispositions of both the mentor and the mentee. Consequently, it is important to be cautious of making uninformed judgments about the nature of a mentoring relationship. I remember vividly one of the experiences that led to this insight. I was working with a group of veteran mentors near the end of the school year, and they were reflecting on some of the ways in which they felt their respective relationships had been successful. One of the women, when it was her turn to share, began describing the fact that she phoned her mentee each morning before school. Before she could finish, several other mentors reacted spontaneously with various expressions of surprise and dismay. The teacher who was sharing reacted immediately, challenging her colleagues to explain their reactions. When no one responded to her challenge, she matter-of-factly described how her mentoring relationship had evolved into what she described as a mother-daughter type relationship. As it turned out, the mentor had lost her husband to illness several years earlier, and both her children were living out of state. The mentee, on the other hand, was living in a new community several hundred miles from her family. Not only did they talk each morning before school, they had dinner together every Thursday night, one week at the mentee's apartment, the next week at the mentor's home. The point of the story is simply this: The relationship was working at both a personal and professional level for both people, and that was all that really mattered.

Mentoring as Pathway to Personal Growth

One of the most common statements you are likely to hear regarding the mentoring of beginning teachers is that the mentors can benefit as much from the relationship as the new teachers. In many cases, such a sentiment is supported by the idea that the veteran teacher might acquire a new instructional idea or practice that the novice teacher learned in college. In other cases, the rationale is more focused on the benefit of having the opportunity to associate with an idealistic beginner who has not been hardened or embittered by some of the difficult realities of professional life. Still others speak simply to how the mentoring relationship can cause one to take a fresh perspective on one's own classroom practices, or serve as the stimulus to reflect on one's own early career experiences. Whereas such explanations all make sense and have obvious value to a veteran teacher, I would like to suggest one additional insight that I have been thinking about a lot in recent months. The idea is simply that veteran teachers who truly dedicate themselves to being good mentors may well have the experience of becoming better persons.

In the process of working to become good mentors—and *process* is the right word—veteran teachers will have many opportunities to experiment with, reflect on, and integrate into their daily lives a constellation of dispositions and behaviors that can enrich their own lives and their interaction with others. Take, for example, the challenge of becoming a more accepting and less judgmental person. There is a strong and quite natural tendency for humans to judge others, and this tendency is often heightened when observing someone perform in an area with which the observer has personal experience, if not expertise. Although clinical assessment may have an important role to play in helping a new teacher develop new technical skills, assessments that are communicated as judgments of inadequacy are almost always counterproductive. Watching a beginning teacher struggle, for example, with behavior management issues can lead a mentor to quickly jump to a number of judgments about the beginning teacher, including her university preparation, her discipline plan, her personal demeanor, her physical appearance, her personality, and the list goes on. Such judgments become particularly insidious when they collect in the mind of the observer and are not recognized for what they are, or for the influences they are likely having on the behavior of the mentor himself. If you believe, as I do, that learning to reserve judgment—or to at least be mindful of when it is beginning to influence one's thoughts and actions—is a habit of mind worth fostering, then you understand what I mean by the claim that being a good mentor can mean being a better person.

THE DEVELOPMENT OF THE MENTORING RELATIONSHIP

Over the years, I have reviewed a number of models that seek to describe how mentoring relationships develop over time. I have studied such models in the hope of finding a cogent way to help prepare mentors for their challenging and important work. Each of the models I have examined offered a slightly different way of thinking about the stages or phases of a mentoring relationship, and I have gleaned one or more important insights from each. On the following pages, I introduce my own model, based on my earlier claim that the quality of a mentoring relationship can vary from low to high, and that the level any such relationship attains is primarily related to the *nature* and *focus* of the conversations that characterize that relationship. See Table 2.1.

Table 2.1 Four Phases of a Mentoring Relationship

Phase	Process	Product
Initiation	Orienting	Mentor and mentee meet one another and form initial impressions. The mentor offers, or the mentee requests, assistance in preparing for the early days of the school year. Problem solving is focused on technical and logistical issues, including finding resources or clarifying policies and procedures.
	Introducing	
Exploration	Accepting	Mentor and mentee begin the process of self-disclosure as they conference about the needs, interests, or goals of the mentee. Early impressions are reinforced or revised as each person moves toward or away from accepting the other. Formal and informal agreements are sometimes negotiated.
	Self-Disclosing	
Collaboration	Sharing	Mentor and mentee act in a trustworthy manner and openly share their personal thoughts and beliefs about a wide range of personal and professional issues. Both become increasingly transparent in their communications. Mentee believes the mentor intends to be a helpful force.
	Trusting	
Consolidation	Respecting	Mentor and mentee appreciate each other on a personal and professional level, and over time develop a strong and enduring sense of positive regard and mutual respect. The relationship merges into one of genuine collegiality and consolidated purpose.
	Appreciating	

In an ideal case, a mentoring relationship develops through four major phases, including *initiation, exploration, collaboration,* and *consolidation.* In other cases, due to a variety of interpersonal and contextual factors, a relationship between a mentor and mentee may arrest in one of the first two phases. In each of the four phases of the relationship, mentors and mentees engage in two basic and somewhat sequential processes that, if successfully engaged, lead to the next phase.

Initiation

The initiation phase of a mentoring relationship consists of two processes, *introduction* and *orientation.* In this first phase, mentors and mentees meet for the first time and begin the relationship-building process. Both parties begin to develop initial impressions of the other. It is not uncommon here for mentees to begin to assess the motives and intentions of the mentor. Similarly, mentors often begin to assess what they perceive to be the mentee's openness to being helped. These initial encounters can range from feeling comfortable to uncomfortable, relaxed to strained, and smooth to awkward. In many cases, these introductions often conclude by focusing on the immediate needs of the mentee. Janice and Colleen, you will remember, never made it to this first level of relationship building because Janice failed to initiate the relationship by introducing herself to Colleen.

Soon after, and sometimes during their first meeting, it is quite common for mentors and mentees to begin focusing on the immediate needs of the mentee, many of which could be classified as orientation needs. For example, mentors often help their mentees find necessary supplies, understand school policies and procedures, or help them in any number of ways prepare for the first days of school. In the best situations, mentoring teams achieve this level before the school year begins, or very early in the school year. Steve helping Tony locate an overhead projector for his classroom would be an example of the kind of help that typically occurs at this level of the relationship.

Exploration

In the exploration phase of the mentoring relationship, mentors and mentees engage in the process of learning about one another. This process is accelerated to the extent that they find the time to meet and engage in conversations in which they begin to reveal their personal biographies, including their past experiences, beliefs, dispositions, and behavioral preferences. Essentially, this is the first step in the process of building a trustworthy relationship. Trust is a function of self-disclosure. Self-disclosure occurs when two people have a shared experience and both parties reveal a personal reaction to that experience. Picture a mentor and mentee sitting to-gether at a beginning-of-the-school-year meeting and hearing the principal articulate her goals for the year. After the meet-ing, the mentor shares with the mentee her belief that the goals are unrealistic. In this case, she has self-disclosed. Next, imagine that on the following day, one of the mentor's colleagues approaches her and says, "So I hear you think the goals are crazy, too." If the mentor had not shared her thoughts with anyone else, she will likely begin to question how trustworthy her mentee is going to be. In this way, and over time, trust between two people is built or shattered. The more personal the self-disclosure, the more value it carries as a matter of trust. Without self-disclosure, trust cannot be established. Some mentor teams never move beyond this level, because one or both of them refuse to engage in the process of self-disclosure, or behave in an untrustworthy manner.

After they have had some initial contact and conversation, the mentoring team faces its first interpersonal crossroad. With their new understandings of each other, will they accept each other in a way that will give their relationship a chance to mature to higher levels? *When* this crossroad is reached depends on many factors, but it is important to note that it is not reached simultaneously. This is important, because if one party begins to send messages of a lack of acceptance, he or she can quickly create reciprocal feelings in the other. This is likely what happened in the story of Carmen and Angie. When Angie discerned that Carmen was not respectful of her personal ideas about teaching, she began to build a wall of defensiveness. In return, Carmen became increasingly aware of that wall, interpreting it as a sign of Angie's immaturity.

Collaboration

In the collaboration phase of the mentoring relationship, mentors and mentees establish trust and begin the process of genuine sharing and collaboration. Once trust is established in a relationship, mentors and mentees begin to take their conversations to deeper and more personal levels, opening the possibility that meaningful dialogue will ensue. If both people remain trustworthy, they will eventually take greater risks in their conversational exchanges. However, one violation of this trust can quickly and often permanently end the development of the relationship. Oftentimes, the offending party never understands what happened. All this person knows is that something has changed in the way the other person is behaving. The mentor who casually shares with his principal that his mentee is struggling with managing student behavior may never know that the principal referred to that conversation in his evaluation conference with the mentee. All he knows for sure is that something has changed in the relationship.

When we become comfortable with another person or group of persons, we feel free to reveal our true selves. We become more transparent in sharing our thoughts, feelings, beliefs, and interpretations. Gone is the tentativeness that often characterizes interactions and communications with people we do not know or trust to have our best interests at heart. At this level, mentors and mentees feel free to share their thoughts and feelings with one another in much the same way as they might with a trusted colleague or friend. Humor, for example, is used in new ways as both parties become comfortable with their own fallibility. At this level, a beginning teacher, for example, might openly share the story of a lesson gone badly. She does so knowing that her mentor will be able to identify with what happened and enjoy the story as well.

Mentors and mentees who reach the collaboration phase of mentoring have jointly created an interpersonal context in which a mutually satisfying relationship can be built and sustained. For many mentors and mentees, reaching this phase of relationship development will be the final phase they will experience.

Consolidation

Some mentoring relationships will, however, mature to a fourth and final phase. At this level mentors and mentees begin to truly appreciate one another, not only as teachers, but as persons as well. The deeper understanding of one another that comes from successfully moving through the preceding levels of relationship building results in feelings of positive regard. The relationship at this level is often described as being friendly in nature. The mentor and mentee enjoy each other's company and look forward to opportunities for meaningful conversation about professional and personal matters.

At the highest level of relationship building, both mentor and mentee arrive at a place of mutual respect that transcends appreciation. Here, for example, mentees may respect their mentors for a variety of reasons, including the knowledge they possess, the caring support they have provided, or the dedication and professionalism they exhibit in their daily practice. In return, mentors may respect their mentees for their enthusiasm and energy, maturity, openness to feedback, or any number of other reasons. How or whether the mentoring relationship continues will depend on a variety of factors that are all part of the serendipity of life itself. Whether they continue to work in the same school and have ongoing dialogue, end up in different states but stay in touch by phone, or never see each other again, really does not matter. For a period of time, they both found satisfaction in sharing their lives as teachers, one more experienced and one just beginning his or her journey. In the story of the beginning teacher Judy and her mentor Beth described in the vignette titled "It's Been Wonderful," we see an example of a relationship with the potential to evolve to this highest level.

QUESTIONS FOR REFLECTION ON MENTORING

Use the following questions to prompt reflection on the content of this chapter and on your current work as a mentor teacher.

- What do you think your beginning teacher would say if I were to ask him or her, "How is it going with your mentor?"
- Did you *show up for the job* of mentoring? If so, how did you do with regard to the following tests:

    o *Intentionality:* Does your beginning teacher sense that you truly intend to be a helpful and therapeutic force in his or her life?
    o *Clarity:* Have you taken the time to speak clearly and specifically with your mentee about the expectations that you hold for yourself as a mentor?
    o *Sincerity:* Does your beginning teacher believe that your communications are honest and well intentioned?

- Have you *stayed on the job* of supporting your beginning teacher? Have you been persistent and tenacious in your efforts? If you are not happy with your answer, what obstacles or setbacks have caused your commitment to slip?
- Have you met the test of time? Are you and your beginning teacher comfortable with the amount of time you are devoting to your relationship?
- If you are *still on the job,* do you believe that your beginning teacher is glad that you are?
- Have you walked your talk with regard to your performance as a mentor teacher? Have you kept your promises? Have you followed through?

- If high-performance mentoring is like a quality conversation, what is the quality of the dialogue you are having with your beginning teacher? Consider the following tests of the good conversation:

  o Have your conversations focused on the deep and meaningful issues of teaching and learning? Or have they been limited to the trivial and superficial?
  o Have they been characterized by acceptance and mutual respect?
  o Have they led to shared meaning?
  o Have they strengthened your relationship?

- If high-performance mentoring is like good teaching, how would you compare your efforts in the classroom with your efforts in your mentoring relationship?
- Finally, after reviewing Table 2.1, what phase do you think your mentoring relationship is in? What can you do to move it to the next higher level?

3

Committing

Unless commitment is made, there are only promises and hopes; but no plans.

—Peter Drucker

There's a difference between interest and commitment. When you're interested in doing something, you do it only when it's convenient. When you're committed to something, you accept no excuses, only results.

—Kenneth Blanchard

In my mentor training programs, typically on the first day of a workshop, I provide prospective mentors with a copy of the High-Performance Mentoring Framework, and then ask them to work in groups to reach consensus on which of the six high-performance mentoring qualities they believe is most important. This is a difficult task, in that each of the qualities can be viewed as fundamentally important. For example, many groups choose *accepting the beginning teacher as a developing person and professional* as being the foundation upon which a good mentoring relationship is built. Others, based perhaps on their own experience, make an argument for *providing hope and optimism for the future.* This initial activity often leads to good small-group discussion followed by whole-group processing in which each team argues for the quality it selected. After the teachers have had a chance to share their thoughts, I offer my own opinion, based on my experiences in supporting and working with both beginning and mentor teachers over the years. For me, it is the issue of *committing to the role of mentor* that is at the very foundation of being a high-performance mentor teacher. Without a significant commitment from the mentor, the other five qualities are unlikely to occur at all. In fact, failing to commit to a mentor-mentee relationship is directly related to the process by which one becomes a low-performing mentor.

As we saw in two of the four beginning teacher vignettes in Chapter 2, commitment was the critical issue in two of the relationships that failed to develop in any meaningful way. In such cases, beginning teachers sometimes find support from department or team members, or other colleagues who serve in the role of *informal mentors.* Such was the case with Colleen, the beginning teacher in the vignette titled "What Mentor?" In other cases, unfortunately, no such relationships develop and beginning teachers find themselves navigating the entry-year waters alone. I believe that this particular phenomenon can be related to the unique nature of school-based mentoring programs, in which veteran practitioners are, in the majority of programs, matched with or are assigned to beginning teachers with whom they have no prior relationship. In other words, no choice is made—either on the part of the mentor or the beginning teacher—to enter the relationship. The mentors may have agreed to serve by enrolling in mentor training, or when they said yes to their building administrator or local mentoring committee. Of course, saying yes to the job does not constitute a commitment. This, as you will recall, was the case with Tony's mentor, Steve, in the vignette "We Haven't Talked for a While." High-performing mentors follow up their agreement to serve with committed action.

COMMITMENT AND INFLUENCE

When interviewing beginning teachers about their personal motivations for wanting to become a teacher, the most common response is that they want to make a difference in the lives of young people. In various ways, they describe how they want to have an impact, how they want to be a positive influence in the lives of their students. High-performance mentors hold the same sentiment with regard to working with beginning teachers. They want to make a difference. Some 20 years ago, when mentoring was a relatively new educational initiative, I spent a good deal of time speaking with school administrators about the value of having a strong, mentor-based, entry-year program in their schools. One night I had just finished speaking to about 100 building principals attending a dinner meeting sponsored by their state association. After my remarks, I invited questions from the audience. As is often the case, instead of a question, I received a rather passionate statement. The principal who spoke first made it clear that my description of what a mentor teacher could do to help a first-year teacher was unrealistic. "My teachers are already working at 110 percent. They don't have the time or the interest to do 10 percent of what you described. If they help them find the supplies they need, or show them how to fill out the forms they have to file, that's enough for them." Of course, I respectfully disagreed, not with the claim that teachers are busy, but rather with the assertion that teachers are not interested in making a more significant impact in the lives of beginning teachers. Despite the fact that today's teachers are facing even greater demands, I know that many are willing to commit themselves to making a difference in the life of a beginning teacher.

As Clawson (1980) made clear, mentoring occurs in an interpersonal context that is based on the *degree of commitment* and *comprehensiveness of influence* on the mentee. High-performance mentors are committed to their work and consequently can, and often do, have comprehensive influence on their mentees. Clawson articulated these dimensions of a mentoring relationship in the form of a two-dimensional graph. I have modified Clawson's original model to reflect my personal interest in the central role that conversation plays in a mentoring relationship. See Figure 3.1.

Figure 3.1 Commitment, Dialogue, and Influence in the Mentoring Relationship

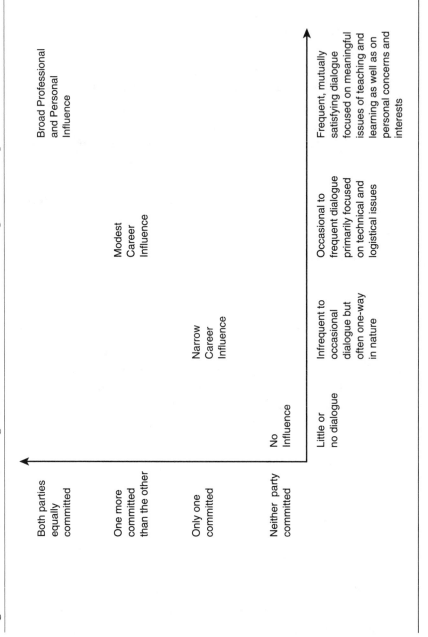

The left-hand, or vertical axis of the graph indicates the degree of commitment present in any given mentoring relationship. Specifically, it treats commitment as occurring at one of four levels, which are functions of the degree of commitment each of the two persons brings to a mentoring relationship. In contrast, the horizontal axis of the graph describes the frequency and nature of the dialogue between mentor and mentee. Finally, the degree of influence that is likely to occur as a result of the mentoring relationship is plotted as a function of commitment and dialogue.

At Level 1 on the commitment scale, neither the mentor nor the mentee demonstrates any real commitment to his or her assigned relationship. As disconcerting as this scenario is, it occurs more often than many educators are willing to admit. In such a situation, little or no dialogue occurs, as is indicated on the horizontal axis of the model. The predictable result is that the relationship, or more accurately the lack thereof, results in no positive influence being exerted on either the mentee or the mentor. If you remember the story titled "What Mentor?" from the preceding chapter that involved a first-year teacher named Colleen and her assigned mentor Janice, it stands as a disheartening example of what happens when commitment is absent and conversation never transpires.

At Level 2 on the commitment scale, only one of the two parties is committed to the relationship. In some cases, it might be the mentor teacher who desires to perform well in hopes of positively influencing the life of the beginning teacher. In other cases, however, it might be the beginning teacher who is committed to working with her mentor in the hopes of improving her performance and being respected by her peers. In such cases where only one of the two parties is committed, dialogue tends to range from infrequent to occasional, but is stifled because only one of the two parties has any real interest in engaging in meaningful conversation. Although some technical assistance might be afforded, there is little significant impact made. The story of a beginning teacher named Tony and his mentor Steve as described in the vignette "We Haven't Talked for a While" serves as an apt example. In this case, Steve was initially committed to helping Tony, and in fact had a vision of their relationship developing in a positive way. Despite an early effort to help Tony equip his classroom, Steve had very limited influence because he believed that it was Tony's responsibility to seek help. If Tony had in fact approached Steve, he would have been happy to help. His commitment, if you will, was conditional. As you recall, Tony chose not to seek Steve's counsel because he enjoyed the autonomy and the opportunity to "figure things out on his own." As a result, Steve's impact was narrow at best.

At Level 3 on the vertical axis, both persons in the relationship are committed to making the relationship work, but one is more committed than the other. This difference in degrees of commitment can occur for the many and varied reasons explicated in this chapter. I recently had a conversation with a new mentor teacher named Sonja, who sensed that she was a lot more committed to helping her mentee than her mentee was to being helped. "I guess it's kind of frustrating, to be honest," she said. "I have waited for 4 years to be assigned a beginning teacher and now that I am working with Christie, I am not sure how it's going." When I asked Sonja what she meant, she explained that it was hard to describe. "I don't exactly know what it is, just a feeling that I have. We attend our district entry-year sessions together and we meet on a pretty regular basis, but sometimes I feel like she is just going through the motions." What was frustrating to Sonja was that she was highly committed to making an impact in the life of her mentee and was not feeling a similar level of commitment in return. As mentioned earlier, such feelings can be reversed, with the beginning teacher being highly committed and frustrated by a lack of similar commitment from his or her mentor. In such scenarios, dialogue does occur with some degree of frequency, but conversations can be somewhat constrained by the imbalance in levels of commitment.

In fact, if you will recall the vignette from Chapter 2 titled "Off to a Bad Start," the mentor Carmen, despite her highly directive approach, was committed to helping her mentee

Angie. She saw her regularly and always had plenty of advice to give and warnings to issue. Angie, the beginning teacher, met with Carmen for fear of being judged uncooperative and did implement some of her ideas, primarily as demonstrations of compliance. In the end, a couple of suggestions proved valuable and Angie incorporated them into her practice. For the most part, however, Angie looked forward to her second year and to Carmen not being a part of her life! Most of the words Carmen had offered would be quickly forgotten.

Finally, at the highest levels of commitment we find what Clawson (1980) described as a true mentoring relationship. In such cases, both mentor and mentee are likely to develop a relationship characterized by frequent and meaningful dialogue that over time focuses on significant issues of teaching and learning, as well as on issues of personal concern and interest. Predictably, this type of relationship is one of significant influence. This influence may be either personal or professional in nature, or both personal and professional. Although it is typical to think of this influence being on the beginning teacher, in a true mentoring relationship the comprehensiveness of influence often is a dynamic, two-way phenomenon in which the mentor teacher is influenced as well.

This model's representation of the important dynamics of commitment, dialogue, and influence provides mentor teachers with a powerful vehicle for reflecting on their personal mentoring relationship. Periodically assessing one's level of commitment or reflecting on the frequency and focus of dialogue in a mentoring relationship can go a long way to keeping a mentor teacher on track. Such reflection, of course, requires that mentors be truthful in their self-assessments and willing to make the necessary changes to have the significant influence that is the ultimate goal of mentoring.

Before discussing the various factors that can affect the commitment of both mentors and mentees, I want to share a thought on how my conception of high-performance mentoring relates to the previously described model. One might be tempted to conclude that high-performance mentoring can occur only at the highest level of commitment and at the highest level of dialogue. From my perspective, this is not necessarily the case. Clearly, high-performance mentors operate at the highest levels of personal commitment, and they do so despite the sometimes lower levels of commitment from their mentees. In such cases, the high-performance mentors persist in their efforts to foster meaningful dialogue despite the covert or overt resistance of the people they are trying to help. In other words, mentors are persistent problem solvers who refuse to allow the attitudes and behaviors of their mentees to deter their mentoring efforts. Like all helping professionals, they understand and accept that the influence they are ultimately able to exert is significantly tied to the mentee's commitment to change and openness to help. Because they possess this foundational understanding, they are willing to reflect on their own behaviors and communications in an effort to find the key or keys that potentially can unlock the mentee's mind and help him or her move to a new place and be cognitively open to assistance and behavioral change. Every mentor would of course love to work with a beginning teacher who is committed to the relationship, open to dialogue, and ready to be influenced. Staying the course when such conditions are not present is a challenge that high-performance mentors are willing to accept.

CAUSES OF LOW MENTOR COMMITMENT

There are a number of factors that can often cause a mentor teacher to exhibit low levels, or only modest levels, of commitment to a mentoring relationship. These factors are complex and personal in nature, and it is consequently difficult to identify all of them. In conducting mentor training workshops, I often ask the participating teachers to help identify those factors that they believe might be the most common causes of low mentor commitment. Here is the list I have constructed from their suggestions. It provides an opportunity for mentors to reflect on their own level of commitment in a mentoring relationship and the various reasons that may cause that commitment to be compromised.

1. Is unclear about the roles and responsibilities of mentoring

2. Lacks an appreciation for the importance of the work

3. Is overwhelmed with personal and professional issues

4. Is unable to accept the mentee's beliefs or behaviors

5. Fears rejection by the mentee

6. Lack of value for mentoring in the school culture

7. Judges the mentee to be highly competent

8. Low commitment from the mentee

Unclear About Mentor's Roles and Responsibilities

It is difficult to commit fully to the role of mentoring if one lacks a clear sense of the roles and responsibilities of the job. Unfortunately, in many schools and districts, this is the case. A mentor is assigned to support a beginning teacher, but without adequate program leadership or appropriate training there are few guideposts to direct the mentor's work. Clearly, some mentors are able to perform at a high level in such an environment because their commitment to being a positive influence is so strong that they are willing and able to create, in essence, their own job description. They follow their personal intuitions about the kinds of things they should do and move forward in a persistent manner, dedicated to making the relationship work. On the other hand, many other mentors placed in such a context struggle with what they should do and, in the end, define their role in a very limited way that often does not result in high levels of influence. Or, worse yet, lacking direction and a clear definition of their roles and responsibilities, they take little or no action at all.

Lacks Appreciation of the Importance of the Work

Sometimes there is a covert—or even overt—belief on the part of mentor teachers that causes them to actually question the need for formal mentor programs. In such cases, there is often an underlying sense that "I struggled through my own first year of teaching and survived, and so will they." Unfortunately, such a belief can insidiously influence a mentor's behavior. The strongest expression of this factor that I have personally experienced came on an evaluation form turned in at the conclusion of a mentor training workshop I had facilitated. The following statement was written in the final section of the evaluation form under "other comments": "As far as I'm concerned this whole mentoring thing is unnecessary and a waste of district resources. I know a lot of good teachers who made it before we began this institutionalized hand-holding."

Overextended in One's Own Life

Another factor that may contribute to low commitment on the part of a mentor is related to the issue of time. In my work with mentor teachers, the single most challenging issue reported by mentor teachers is "finding the time." Sometimes this problem is the result of the fact that those teachers who are asked to mentor are those who are successful in many other aspects of their professional lives. In many cases, they are people capable of handling multiple tasks who have a history of finishing any jobs that they begin. It takes a high level of commitment to function effectively as a mentor when one has so many other competing responsibilities. Clearly, there is much truth in the notion that people generally find the time to do the things that they most value. In fact, the amount of time that one spends on any particular endeavor is one of the strongest measures of one's personal value system. Perhaps this explains why some of the busiest teachers, those serving their school and district in many other capacities, still manage to build a meaningful mentoring relationship and have high degrees of influence on their beginning teachers.

Although it is true that some mentors are able to manage many competing responsibilities and function effectively, others are not so successful because they feel overextended in their own lives to a point where they are psychologically or emotionally tired and find it difficult to carve out the time necessary to maintain their commitment to mentoring. The perhaps overused story about helping others in an airplane when oxygen masks are deployed applies here. When the flight attendant advises passengers to first put on their own oxygen masks before attempting to assist others who are in need, such as a child or an elderly person, we are reminded of how challenging it is to help another when one is in need of help oneself.

Unable to Accept the Mentee's Beliefs

Sometimes mentor teachers discover that their beginning teacher operates personally and professionally from a belief system very different from their own. It is generally true in human behavior that people tend to gravitate toward and connect with others who are like themselves. Discovering, for example, that a beginning teacher holds an educational philosophy very different from one's own can be both a problem and an opportunity. Clearly, it is an opportunity to the mentor teacher who is open-minded, accepting, and willing to have meaningful and honest dialogue about that philosophy, and perhaps even how it differs from her own. In contrast, it is clearly a problem if the mentor covertly or overtly rejects the beginning teacher because of these differences. In such cases, there is a tendency on the part of the mentor to move away, to back off, eventually exhibiting little or no commitment to the relationship.

Fears Rejection by the Mentee

Teaching is a highly personal and emotionally demanding job. Even the most successful teachers experience periods of fatigue and ennui. At such times, it is not uncommon to be especially sensitive to the opinions and behaviors of others, be they students, colleagues, or supervisors. A mentor teacher experiencing such an emotional state is in a vulnerable position. Reaching out to extend an offer of help is risky business when you believe that your offer may be rejected or simply disregarded. Facing such an outcome, some mentors choose, consciously or unconsciously, to reduce their commitment to the relationship.

Lack of Appreciation for Mentoring in the School Culture

Mentoring takes places in the context of school culture. In some schools, there is a sense that mentoring is an important function. In such a school culture, mentors are respected for their work and mentoring is a celebrated and valued enterprise. In contrast, in other schools, many teachers view formal mentoring as simply the latest fad. Such schools often lack a positive history of mentoring in which mentor and beginning teachers are publicly recognized and supported by other staff members. In such settings, it is easy for mentor teachers to exhibit low commitment because they know that their peers and administrators hold relatively low expectations for their work as mentors.

Judges the Mentee to Be Highly Competent

One of the most common factors leading to low commitment in a mentoring relationship occurs when mentors judge their beginning teachers to be highly competent. Impressed with their knowledge and skill, mentors decide that there is little or nothing they can do to help. I am surprised by how frequently I hear this sentiment expressed. From my perspective, it is difficult to imagine a beginning teacher who could not profit from working with a caring and committed mentor. Granted, beginning teachers vary widely with regard to their knowledge and skill and some are quite advanced in both their confidence and competence. The challenge for the high-performance mentor is to help such individuals move to even higher levels of professional practice. This can be an intimidating thought if the mentor cannot imagine how to foster such growth. Lacking such vision, it becomes easier to conclude that "they will be fine without me."

Low Commitment From the Mentee

One of the most powerful factors contributing to low mentor commitment occurs when the mentor senses low commitment on the part of the beginning teacher. "I am not going to knock myself out trying to help someone who acts like they could care less about what I have to say" was the way one new mentor explained his decision to let his beginning teacher "find his own way." As is typically the case, these sentiments were shared with a good deal of emotion, including a mix of frustration and anger. Such emotions are understandable, but when left unchecked, typically lead to the end of any meaningful commitment to the relationship. In such cases, high-performance mentors monitor and accept their emotional response to the situation but then move on to a thoughtful examination of what might be causing the beginning teacher to behave in this way. Included in these reflections is an honest assessment of their own behaviors, as well as the behaviors of the mentee. Then, like good teachers frustrated with the reluctant or resistant student, mentors plan their next action aimed at building the relationship anew.

LOW MENTEE COMMITMENT

As the commitment, dialogue, and influence model presented earlier reminds us, high-impact mentoring can only occur in an interpersonal context in which both people are committed to making the relationship work. Consequently, for every mentoring relationship that fails because of low mentor commitment, there is likely one that fails because of low commitment on the part of the beginning teacher. I have asked beginning teachers to help me understand what factors might cause this to happen. Here are their thoughts:

1. Strong desire to be an autonomous professional

2. Fear of being judged inadequate

3. Believes asking for help is a sign of incompetence

4. Unable to accept the mentor's beliefs or behaviors

5. Does not want to be a burden to another professional

6. Lacks appreciation for the complexity of teaching

7. Judges the mentor to be uncaring

8. Low commitment from the mentor

The Desire to Be an Autonomous Professional

Many novice teachers begin their careers with a strong desire to prove themselves to themselves. Following years of university classes, supervised fieldwork, and an extensive student teaching or internship experience, many beginning teachers see their first year of teaching as a time when they will be able to operate independently, making autonomous decisions about their practice. For those who have strong dispositions in this direction, there often is a hesitancy to engage fully in the mentoring relationship. Prior to meeting their mentor, there is already a sense that one is not needed. After meeting the mentor, such feelings may continue to grow, especially if the beginning teacher senses that the mentor is fully committing to his or her role and seems intent on being involved in the mentee's first year of practice. Responding to such feelings, some beginning teachers move away from the mentor, sending signals of disinterest. Such signals are then interpreted by the mentor as a lack of respect, or of unwarranted overconfidence. In either case, one response of mentors receiving such signals is to lower their commitment as well.

Fear of Being Judged Inadequate

When beginning teachers begin to sense that a mentor has formed a negative impression of their professional performance, there is a natural tendency to reduce their commitment to the mentoring relationship. Many beginning teachers are highly sensitive to what they perceive to be unfair or uninformed judgments of their practice. Predictably, they have a strong desire or need to be accepted into the school community and to be validated for their efforts, if not their actual performance. One of the most common defense mechanisms is to simply reduce one's commitment to the mentoring relationship. This phenomenon often occurs in programs where mentors are required to conduct classroom observations of beginning teachers, but are not adequately trained in feedback and conferencing techniques designed to defeat the interpersonal demon called defensiveness.

Believes Asking for Help
Is a Sign of Incompetence

One of the most common reasons for low commitment on the part of beginning teachers is a strong sense that seeking help, advice, or support from another is a sign of weakness or incompetence. As has been well documented, beginning teachers operate in what Fuller (1969) described as the Survival Stage, a developmental period where their driving concern is acceptance and their focus is on self-related issues. For some beginning teachers, this focus on self takes the form of a strong need to preserve an image of confidence. Although this may indicate an immature disposition, it nonetheless is developmentally common. For example, the beginning teacher who finds herself unable to manage the behavior of her fourth graders may believe that to admit her inability to do so would be to risk her reputation with her mentor. Facing such a possibility, she chooses to try to solve the problem on her own.

Unable to Accept the Mentor's Beliefs or Behaviors

In some cases, beginning teachers recognize that the beliefs they hold about good teaching, or even about students, are quite different from those of their mentors. This is troubling for them, especially if they begin to characterize the beliefs of the mentor as antiquated or unenlightened. If an attempt to talk about the perceived differences is made, and subsequently rejected by the mentor, a certain uncomfortable distance is often created. In some cases, this takes the form of an unspoken agreement not to talk about those things about which mentor and mentee know they do not agree. In other cases, the interpersonal disconnect is more dramatic and one or both parties move to polarized positions where the relationship dies.

Not Wanting to Burden Another Professional

Schools are busy places and teachers are busy people. For the new observer, the flurry of activity and lack of time appear to be the common workplace condition. Observing other teachers working in such a climate, many beginning teachers are reluctant to seek help, even from a formally designated mentor, for fear that they will be a burden on that person. Instead of asking for help, they try to find their own solutions to problems. When those solutions fail to work, they often begin to further doubt themselves.

Lacks Appreciation for the Complexity of Teaching

Teaching is a complex activity that requires a knowledge base and skill set that develop over time and in practice. Many beginning teachers, despite having just completed their university preparation, approach the first year of teaching with the belief that teaching is a simpler enterprise than it really is.

For beginning teachers with such a perspective, there is often a lack of interest in engaging in conversations about teaching. They have a narrow conception of what constitutes teaching well and they believe that they are doing so. Why complicate matters by talking about someone else's perspective, someone else's interpretation?

Judges the Mentor to Be Uncaring

People tend to learn the most from those individuals whom they respect and who communicate warmth and caring. When beginning teachers encounter a mentor who fails to communicate warmth and a true, caring intention to help, it is not unusual for the mentee to move to a position of low commitment. In the mentee's view, to commit to such a relationship is to put the mentee at risk of being judged inadequate, which—at that point in a developing career—is one of his or her greatest fears.

Low Mentor Commitment

Finally, nothing more quickly moves a beginning teacher into not committing to a mentoring relationship than the sense that the mentor is not committed. "Why should I invest my time and energy in trying to work and build a relationship with someone who shows no evidence that he or she is truly committed to helping me?"

COMMITMENT INDICATORS

On the high-performance mentoring matrix presented in Chapter 1, the subpoints that follow each of the six qualities are presented as examples of the kinds of behaviors that are representative of each respective quality. The list for each quality is not intended to be a comprehensive reporting of all of the behaviors that might be associated with that quality. Instead, the bulleted list represents sample behaviors that can help mentors reflect on their practice with regard to each of the high-performance mentoring qualities. The five indicators for *Commits to the Roles and Responsibilities of Mentoring* are:

1. Dedicates time to meet with the mentee

2. Persists in efforts to help the mentee despite obstacles or setbacks

3. Maintains congruence between mentoring words and actions

4. Attends meetings and professional development programs related to mentoring

5. Models self-reflection and self-assessment as hallmarks of professionalism

Dedicates Time to Meet With the Mentee

A mentor teacher's commitment to find the time to meet with his mentee is one of the most fundamental ways in which commitment is expressed in a mentoring relationship. In my own work with mentors, it is clear that the most commonly reported problem of mentors is finding the time to devote to the relationship. As mentioned earlier, however, high-performing mentors find the time by creatively seeking out the solution that can work in the given context. Some mentors, for example, given the constraints of teaching schedules, find it necessary to meet before or after school. Others make extensive use of e-mail and phone calls to maintain contact with their mentee. Many mentors have shared that it is important to set appointments with their beginning teachers. Some establish a regular meeting time each week, or perhaps even every day. Such meetings need not be long, as a lot can often be accomplished in a short conversation. If there is a complex issue or problem to be dealt with, and time permits, the meeting can be extended. If not, a more appropriate time can be arranged. The point here is that there is no best way to manage time in a mentoring relationship. What is essential is an understanding on the mentor's part that without adequate time, the relationship cannot and will not flourish. Mentors who are unwilling to problem-solve the time challenge severely limit the impact they are likely to have on the beginning teacher.

Persists in Efforts to Assist the Mentee Despite Obstacles and Setbacks

In any human relationship where one person intends to help another, persistence is a key to success. In any mentoring relationship there will likely be moments that cause the mentor to question the mentee's behavior. Take, for example, a mentor who is concerned because her mentee has cancelled the last two meetings that she has scheduled with her. A mentor's first reaction might be to judge the beginning teacher as being irresponsible or disrespectful. Such judgments, if unrecognized and unresolved, can cause commitment to wane. A high-performing mentor teacher, on the other hand, would see the two missed meetings as an opportunity for a conversation about how the beginning teacher is managing her own time and the multiple responsibilities she is trying to fulfill. In other words, the concern can be expressed in a caring way that can potentially lead to good conversation that may reveal deeper problems that can be addressed.

Another common obstacle that some mentors must navigate is the realization that their mentee does not always follow their advice or suggestions. Take, for example, the case of a beginning teacher who expresses concern about the behavior of one of her students and engages the mentor in dialogue about possible solutions. During the meeting, the mentor and mentee negotiate an agreement that the beginning teacher should take two important steps, namely, contacting the parents and notifying the school counselor. Several days later, when the mentor inquires about how it's going and whether or not the beginning teacher has done the work she agreed to, it becomes apparent that neither task was completed. Again, there is a danger here that the mentor moves to a position of reduced commitment, feeling as if her time had been wasted in having the conversation. If left unresolved, such feelings can seriously compromise the relationship as the mentor teacher moves away feeling rejected. In contrast, a high-performing mentor, upon hearing the report, might ask, "Have you decided to go in a different direction? Has the behavior improved? Is there anything I can do to help? Would you like to meet again to continue our conversations?" Such questions reflect a commitment to persist on behalf of the beginning teacher and place the focus appropriately on the beginning teacher and her problems, as opposed to the feelings of the mentor.

Maintains Congruence Between Words and Actions

High-performing mentor teachers are people whose daily actions in the mentoring relationship are congruent with their beliefs and the promises they have made to the beginning teacher. Early in a mentoring relationship, they clearly express their intentions to help the beginning teacher, and in many cases, specifically describe the ways in which they intend to help. Or, they ask the beginning teacher what kinds of help he or she would prefer. One of the most important ways in which commitment is expressed in a mentoring relationship is through congruent words and actions. Lacking such congruence, beginning teachers begin to doubt the sincerity of their mentor's words and often move to a position of reduced commitment. Such movement unfortunately often results in a reciprocal pattern in which, sensing the reduced commitment on the part of the beginning teacher, the mentor reduces her commitment as well. Consequently, mentors are well advised to be careful about what they say they will do, promising only what they are confident they can deliver.

Attends Meetings and
Professional Development Programs

In most schools and school districts, mentoring relationships occur in a program context that includes the requirement that mentors or mentees attend meetings, workshops, or support sessions. Sometimes the expectation is that mentors and mentees will attend such programs together. In other cases, meetings are tailored to meet the needs of either mentors or mentees. Regardless of the nature of the meeting, mentors must be aware that mentees tend to view such meetings as an expression of the mentor's commitment. Granted, both mentors and mentees are busy and have many competing responsibilities. Of course, there are occasions when other responsibilities take priority. In such cases, it is important that mentors inform their beginning teachers why they will not be able to attend, and express regret. Far too many times I have facilitated sessions intended for beginning teachers and their mentors, and have felt the awkwardness associated with first-year teachers attending such a meeting and sitting alone while others are engaged in conversation. Sometimes when I ask the beginning teachers if their mentor is coming they will have a good explanation, and it is clear that the mentee understands. Unfortunately, in other cases, the answer—or lack thereof—speaks volumes.

Models Self-Reflection and Self-Assessment

One of the keys to maintaining commitment in a mentoring relationship is the mentor's willingness to self-monitor his or her commitment. It is very important to ask periodically: "Where is my commitment level? Is it strong and growing? Is it modest and weakening? Is it weak and slipping?" Whereas questioning oneself in this way can be difficult as one faces unpleasant realities, it is the only way I know to ensure that one is monitoring one's commitment and hopefully considering appropriate responses. Mentors who fail to reflect in this way can, over time, slip into behaviors that are not consistent with committed service.

QUESTIONS FOR REFLECTION ON COMMITTING

Use the following questions to prompt reflection on the content of this chapter and on your current work as a mentor teacher.

- As Ken Blanchard (1993) might ask: Are you *interested* in mentoring, or are you *committed*?
- Reflecting on your mentoring relationship, can you identify a *specific plan* you currently have for helping your beginning teacher? As Peter Drucker has suggested, commitment leads to plans, not just promises.
- Where would you plot your commitment, and the commitment of your beginning teacher, on the vertical axis of the Commitment, Dialogue, and Influence Model?
- Reflecting on the frequency and nature of the conversations you are having with your mentee, how would you characterize the dialogue in your mentoring relationship using the horizontal axis of the Commitment, Dialogue, and Influence Model?
- If you are not satisfied with an honest assessment of your level of commitment, what factors may have contributed to that level? Reflecting on the factors identified by teachers and reported in this chapter should facilitate that process.
- If you are not content with the level of commitment you are sensing from your beginning teacher, what factors may be at work? Begin with a thoughtful review of the low-commitment factors identified by beginning teachers. Can you identify a personal strategy aimed at increasing your mentee's commitment?
- If things continue as they are in your mentoring relationship, what degree of influence do you believe you will have on your beginning teachers?
- If commitment is foundational to high-performance mentoring, how are you performing with regard to the following indicators of commitment?

- o Are you finding the time to meet with your mentee?
- o Are you persisting in your mentoring efforts despite the obstacles and setbacks you will surely encounter?
- o Have you maintained congruence between your mentoring words and actions?
- o Have you made an honest effort to attend meetings and professional development sessions that may be part of your mentoring program?
- o Have you engaged in self-reflection and self-assessment with regard to your work as a mentor teacher?

- Finally, do you truly believe that you can make a positive difference in the personal and professional life of a beginning teacher?

4

Accepting

We cannot change anything until we accept it.
Condemnation does not liberate, it oppresses.

—Carl Jung

No matter who says what, you should accept it with a
smile and do your own work.

—Mother Teresa

When you criticize me, I intuitively dig in to defend
myself. When you accept me like I am, I suddenly am
willing to change.

—Carl Rogers

One of the greatest challenges in the process of mentoring is the challenge of acceptance. Again, this is especially true in school-based mentoring programs where mentor and mentee relationships are typically assigned, rather than self-selected. In other words, prior to the relationship being created there is no precondition of acceptance. Instead, two adults, often with little or no personal understanding of one another, are paired or matched in what is hoped to be a helping relationship. Whether the relationship actually turns out to be a helpful one largely depends on the capacity of each individual to accept the other. Whereas it is of course important for the mentee to accept the mentor, it is critical that the mentor accept the mentee. In fact, this dynamic is such that if the mentor fails to communicate acceptance, the odds are that the mentee will fail to accept the mentor, and the relationship will likely be arrested at a low level, or fail to develop at all. One need only reflect on the story of Carmen and Angie in Chapter 2 to be reminded how the failure to communicate acceptance of the mentee and her ideas can become a toxic force in a developing relationship. When Carmen's meeting with Angie began with criticism and directives, Angie quickly sensed that her own professional thinking was not being accepted.

THE CHALLENGE OF ACCEPTANCE

There are many reasons why communicating acceptance is a challenge. First, one cannot communicate acceptance of another if one has not internally adopted an accepting perspective. And for many mentor teachers, this is not an easy thing to do. It is not easy because human beings have a strong tendency to judge. For most of us, judging comes as naturally as breathing, and this is part of the problem. Unless a person is ill with some type of respiratory ailment, breathing just happens, with little conscious attention. Biologically speaking, breathing is for the most part an automatic function. On the other hand, we are all aware that by focusing on our breathing we can alter its automatic nature. We can breathe deeper, faster, slower, or—if we choose—not at all. In many ways, judging people, places, and things is like breathing. It can be and often is an automatic function that serves many useful purposes. An aggressive driver passes us on the freeway and then zigs and zags between several other cars at a high rate of speed, and we judge the person to be road-raging and slow down to create some distance between us and what we anticipate might become a multicar accident. Whether the other person actually was road-raging or was trying to race his pregnant wife to the hospital does not matter. We simply acquired some external input, made a judgment, and adjusted our behavior accordingly. This process of judgment was just as automatic as the one taken by another driver who was personally offended by being cut off and decided to give chase so that he could get even, by hopefully cutting off the offending driver.

For mentor teachers, and for any person desiring to communicate acceptance of another, the key is learning to develop a heightened awareness of one's judging. Just as athletes are trained to monitor their breathing, mentors can learn to monitor their judgments. This process of the metacognitive monitoring of one's judgments is a highly personal process, and each person must develop his or her own technique. One writer, for example, describes taking what he calls his mental helicopter ride to the ceiling, where he can observe not only his behaviors but monitor his emotional state as well. Personally, I am a fan of tree houses and in recent years have created my own observation point in an imaginary tree house where I frequently use the words, "Isn't that interesting?" as my way of assessing my own thoughts and behaviors, as well as the thoughts and behaviors of those I am seeking to help. I find these words helpful because they provide the starting point for altering my own behavior. Here's a recent example of how this process works that is related to the larger issue of acceptance in helping relationships.

Finding Your Tree House

Driving home from work one afternoon, I was listening to a popular talk show host whose show I always assumed was aimed at helping callers who phoned in to share some personal dilemma. On this particular afternoon, a young woman called in to share some feelings she was struggling with that had to do with her decision to have an abortion several years earlier when she was in college. In just a few seconds, it became apparent that the caller was very upset and was genuinely reaching out for help. The words "despondent" and "desperate" seemed apt descriptions of her emotional state.

I was not prepared for the host's reply. It was, in my judgment, unwarranted, irresponsible, and totally inappropriate given the caller's vulnerable state. It was clear to me that she was experiencing a lot of guilt around her decision and was reaching out for someone to help her deal with those feelings. What she received instead was an angry diatribe condemning her for making such an immoral decision. Somewhere in the middle of her response, the host asked an angry rhetorical question. When she did not receive a response, she sarcastically commented something to the effect that "the truth hurts and apparently" the caller was "not ready to hear it." I was so angry with the host's insensitivity that I pulled off the road fully intending to call the show and take her to task on national radio.

Sitting in my car and listening for the call-in number, I suddenly realized that it was time for a trip to the tree house. Becoming the observer, I quickly recognized that I was in an emotional state triggered by my own judgments of the conversation. By the way, those judgments had nothing to do with any personal stance on the controversial issue of abortion. Rather, they had to do with my personal beliefs about what constitutes a helping relationship. At that point in time, it was interesting to me that I had allowed myself to become so emotionally involved with such a remote problem. Somewhere, a young woman was in a deep state of self-judgment about a decision she had made years before. Somewhere, a talk show host had no doubt moved on to her next caller, or to the next commercial, and I was sitting alongside the road trying to right what I perceived to be a wrong. Isn't that interesting? After a few seconds, I closed my cell phone, turned off the radio, checked my side view mirror, and resumed my drive home, processing the experience in light of Rogers's (1958) theory of client-centered counseling.

RELATIONSHIP OF ACCEPTANCE
AND UNDERSTANDING

Carl Rogers, the renowned American psychologist and developer of client-centered counseling, was one of the most influential voices in the development of therapeutic counseling techniques. Rogers (1958) described a helping relationship as "a relationship in which at least one of the parties has the intent of promoting the growth, development, maturity, improved functioning, and improved coping with life of the other." He believed that in order to promote such growth it was essential that counselors be congruent, empathic, and respectful in their interactions with clients, and that such qualities were necessary and sufficient for a relationship to be truly helpful.

Speaking of the important relationship between acceptance and understanding, Rogers (1961) wrote,

> Acceptance does not mean much until it involves understanding. It is only as I understand the feelings and thoughts which seem so horrible to you, or so weak, or so sentimental, or so bizarre—it is only as I see them as you see them, and accept them and you, that you feel really free to explore and grow as an independent person. (p. 34)

In some respects, adopting such an understanding and accepting perspective requires that mentors develop multiple lenses for viewing the lives of beginning teachers. The more one knows about beginning teachers, the more likely one is to understand and accept the diverse and idiosyncratic thoughts, feelings, and behaviors that make them so interesting to observe, and so challenging to help. Beginning teachers are wildly different from one another. At the same time, they are alike. Adopting a "different but alike" perspective on beginning teachers is a good way for mentors to begin to foster a more accepting and understanding disposition. Consider the following five statements as examples of such a disposition.

1. All beginning teachers have problems, but their problems are as different as are their personal responses to those problems.

2. All beginning teachers are being socialized, but their internal processing of that experience is different at the intersection of personal biography and socializing forces.

3. All beginning teachers have developmental concerns, but those concerns vary in intensity and length of time experienced.

4. All beginning teachers are learners, but have different needs depending on the nature of the challenges they encounter and the level of skill they possess to meet those challenges.

5. All beginning teachers are adults, but their levels of commitment and cognition can vary independently of their ages.

Each of the above statements is based on a research-based or theoretical perspective that can help mentor teachers develop deeper understanding and greater acceptance of the beginning teachers they are seeking to help. The vignettes that follow are based on actual experiences I have had in talking with mentor teachers. They will be used to introduce a further explication of the five "different but alike" statements.

Common Problems

Cathy was in her mid-thirties when she began her first year of teaching in a suburban elementary school, where she was assigned to teach fourth grade. Doris, a 20-year veteran teacher, was assigned to mentor Cathy. I was pilot testing some new beginning teacher assessment protocols for the state department of education and consequently had the opportunity to visit with Doris on several occasions, and to observe in Cathy's classroom. The first time I met privately with Doris, she expressed grave concerns about Cathy's "naïve and idealistic" beliefs about individualizing instruction. "It's unbelievable; I have never seen anything quite like it. She is hell-bent on having an individual learning plan for every student, every day." Doris went on to explain her efforts to convince Cathy that such a commitment was unrealistic and would be impossible to maintain over time. "I've tried repeatedly to tell her that it isn't healthy to be spending as much time as she is on planning. I think it's starting to affect her health already. She is not getting the sleep she needs." When I asked Doris what she was planning to do next to help Cathy, she explained that she planned to continue trying to convince her to slow down and not hold herself to such high standards. "It's obvious to me she is going to crash at some point. Nobody can maintain the pace she is on. I don't care who you are, or who you are trying to impress."

A number of studies have revealed that beginning teachers tend to experience similar or common problems. One of the most frequently cited papers was written by Veenman (1984), who conducted a meta-analysis of more than 80 studies that had previously explored the problems of beginning teachers using divergent methodologies. The result of the analysis was a list of 24 commonly reported problems, presented in terms of their frequency of report. One of the activities that I frequently employ in training mentors is to ask them to work in teams to try to identify and rank-order what they think the top eight problems were, as reported by Veenman's research. Although they typically do well in predicting classroom discipline as the most common problem, they almost always fail to identify motivating students and dealing with individual differences as numbers two and three, respectively. These very student-focused problems were likely the ones that Cathy felt particularly compelled to solve and that Doris had a difficult time understanding. If she had been more aware that many beginning teachers enter the profession highly committed to creating engaging classroom environments in which they imagine making a difference in the lives of each of their students, she perhaps could have been more accepting of Cathy's extraordinary efforts in that regard.

By the way, prospective mentors tend to do a pretty good job of identifying the other problems on Veenman's (1984) list. Once they have seen the list, they frequently acknowledge that these are many of the same problems that they continue to confront in their own practice. What is different, of course, is that they have had years to develop not only the technical strategies to deal with them, but the coping skills to manage the emotional side effects as well. High-performance mentors are mindful of this reality and are not shocked or surprised when their beginning teachers react to these problems with a range of efficacy and emotion. They accept them where they are, empathically acknowledge the reality of the problem being experienced, and respectfully endeavor to understand the problem from their point of view. With such support, beginning teachers become more open to help and more committed to their personal and professional growth.

Here are the top eight problems as identified by Veenman (1984).

1. Classroom discipline

2. Motivating students

3. Dealing with individual differences

4. Assessing student work

5. Relationships with parents

6. Planning and organizing class work

7. Lack of materials and supplies

8. Students' personal problems

Implications for Mentoring

What is important to remember as a mentor teacher is that virtually all beginning teachers encounter and react to these problems in very different ways. One year, you may mentor a beginning teacher who is devastated by her inability to manage student behavior. The next year, you mentor someone who manages student behavior like a veteran, but is highly committed to creating performance-based evaluations for her students, and is frustrated by their lack of interest in her authentic assessments.

Socialized and Socializing

A great deal has been written about the socialization of teachers. For an excellent and comprehensive review of that literature, I recommend the paper by Zeichner and Gore (1990). One particularly helpful way of thinking about the socialization of beginning teachers was advanced by Lacey (1977). Historically, the dominant view of socialization was one in which beginning teachers were seen as being cajoled and molded into shapes acceptable within their schools. Lacey challenged this "functionalist" model of teacher socialization with a more "interactional" one, in which the personal biography of the beginning teacher was viewed as interacting with the socializing forces that were in place in the school environment. In this view, teachers are seen as having the ability to create their own professional identities and adopt their own perspectives in interaction with the socializing forces exerted by students, colleagues, administrators, previous teachers, and others. Lacey identified three types of social strategies—*strategic redefinition*, *strategic compliance*, and *internalized adjustment*.

Strategic Redefinition

Jerry was in the second semester of his senior year of college when he attended a job fair and impressed the principal of a rural high school not far from his hometown. Within a month, he had signed his first contract to teach high school social studies. Barb, a departmental colleague with 8 years of experience, accepted the job to mentor Jerry through his first year. I met Barb when I was hired to conduct mentor training for her county's educational service center. At the morning break on our first day of training, Barb came up to ask my advice on what to do when a beginning teacher "thinks he knows it all." When I responded jokingly that "I guess it depends on whether he really does," she made it clear that this was not the case. "He can't stop talking about all the great things he is doing and how they are best practices. Now everybody in the building can't stop talking about how arrogant he is." When I acknowledged how frustrating this must be for her, she said she was at a loss about what to do. "It's kind of hard to try and help someone who acts like you are the one who needs the help. I tried to have a conversation the other day about group work and he recommended two books I should read."

If Barb had been aware of Lacey's (1977) framework for thinking about the social strategies that beginning teachers employ, she may have understood that Jerry was exhibiting a social strategy Lacey called *strategic redefinition*. Individuals such as Jerry seem to be relatively unconstrained by the opinions of others and manifest a strong sense of self-confidence. They tend, if you will, to march to the beat of their own drummer, and don't necessarily care if others are hearing that drumbeat. Mentors charged with supporting the strategic redefiner are frequently confronted with complaints from colleagues and with their own sense of frustration about how to help someone who seems so confident in their own skin. The real challenge for mentors of strategic redefiners is to avoid the temptation to label or reject such mentees because they appear disinterested in or even critical of the ideas of others. As discussed earlier, a more accepting approach would be to acknowledge and accept the beginning teacher's behavior and begin crafting appropriate strategies. The self-talk might sound something like this: "Okay, this is very interesting. I think Jerry is behaving like a strategic redefiner. How can I build and maintain a relationship with him that might be potentially helpful?" Here are some possible responses a mentor teacher might take in such a situation. They are presented here only as examples of some of the types of responses that may prove helpful.

1. Express interest in the beginning teacher's thinking by asking him to share instructional ideas and resources.

2. Ask the beginning teacher to show you examples of student work, because you are interested in seeing the impact of his efforts.

3. Through journals, books, or Internet research, learn about the professional topics the beginning teacher seems to be most interested in.

4. Ask the beginning teacher what new areas of professional development he would like to pursue.

5. Be open to the possibility that the beginning teacher's performance could be as good as his claims. And, be open to the possibility that it might not.

6. Be patient. Sometimes such behaviors run their course over time as the beginning teacher is gradually humbled by discovering how much he or she does not know.

Strategic Compliance

Of course, the next time Barb mentors a beginning teacher, she may experience someone who Lacey (1977) would describe as "strategically compliant." Such individuals tend to comply with an authority figure's definition of a situation while they retain private reservations. Let's imagine that when Barb was discussing cooperative learning with Jerry, she shared that she rarely uses it in her classroom because she feels it is unfair to high-achieving students, and too time-consuming. Jerry, as a strategic redefiner, recommended that she read a couple of books on cooperative learning. In contrast, the strategically compliant beginning teacher, despite a personal belief in the power of cooperative learning, may well decide not to practice it for fear of offending Barb. In other words, he would retain his personal beliefs about the power of cooperative learning, but decide to wait until his second year to implement cooperative learning methods; hence the term strategically compliant. Strategic compliance is a popular strategy for student teachers because they often recognize the need to comply with the preferences of their cooperating teachers. This phenomenon is, of course, accelerated by the fact that the cooperating teacher may have significant input on the student teacher's grade or final evaluation. In the case of beginning teachers, the process can be accelerated not by a fear of a low grade or poor letter of recommendation, but instead by the need to be accepted by their mentor, their principal, or any other person they feel it is important to please. Here are some examples of strategies for dealing with strategically compliant beginning teachers:

1. Early in the relationship, seek to draw out their basic beliefs about what constitutes good teaching. Then, let them know that you are interested in helping them put those ideas to work in their classroom.

2. Look for opportunities to validate and reinforce their ideas about teaching and learning.

3. Be attentive to how they react to other authority figures and the influence they might exert.

4. Remind them that there are many right ways to carry out many professional practices, and that it is important that they experiment with the practices that they value.

5. Periodically ask them how they are doing with regard to some professional practice you know they were originally committed to trying.

6. Avoid sending strong messages that communicate your disapproval of professional practices that are legitimate, but which you personally choose not to employ.

7. Remember that beginning teachers are very vulnerable in terms of their job status and that being strategically compliant can sometimes be a very intelligent thing to do.

Internalized Adjustment

Finally, there is a third social strategy not uncommon to beginning teachers. In the Lacey (1977) framework, it is known as "internalized adjustment." In the situation described above, where Barb expressed her own serious concerns about cooperative learning, a third beginning teacher might well accept Barb's opinions on cooperative learning, abandon his personally held beliefs, and internally adjust to the ideas of his mentor. Such teachers actually adopt the values in place in the new situation, believing that the authority figure must be right. In this case, the new teacher might reason that Barb has much more experience and should know what will and will not work in this particular school. I am particularly concerned about beginning teachers who are quick to internally adjust to the constraints present in the workplace. The socializing forces at work in schools are often powerful influences that can move such teachers to adopt professional beliefs and practices that are not always in their best interest, or in the best interest of the children they teach. I have seen veteran teachers, administrators, and mentors profoundly influence the beliefs of beginning teachers in ways that were not helpful, and in some cases harmful. In its most insidious form, such influence comes from authority figures with personal agendas or political motives that really have no good reason for being exerted on beginning teachers and have little or nothing to do with student learning. Here are a few practical suggestions for helping mentees who manifest a disposition toward internalized adjustment:

1. Talk openly with them about the value of their professional beliefs and theories and the role they play, not only in learning to teach, but throughout their teaching lifetime. You cannot help someone manifest their personal beliefs about good teaching if you do not know what they are.

2. Be explicit with them about your concern that they may be internalizing the beliefs of others without giving their own belief system sufficient time to be tested in practice. Done tactfully, this will be perceived as a compliment.

3. If you are in a setting where you and your mentee hear a veteran teacher or administrator express a strong

belief about some professional issue, look for a timely opportunity to discuss the issue with the mentee.

4. Share your own regrets of how you abandoned a personal belief about good teaching prematurely, only to discover later that your initial belief was important and worth defending.

5. Whenever possible, validate their beliefs and congruent practices by pointing out how they are related to what is empirically known about good teaching or about how children learn.

6. Share your own beliefs about teaching and learning and how they evolved over time and have been shaped by experience.

Hopefully, you agree that mentor teachers can be challenged by beginning teachers employing any of the three social strategies. What is important for mentors is to make the effort, through conversation and thoughtful observation, to better understand their beginning teachers from this socialization perspective. The purpose here is not to label them, but to better understand and more fully accept them for who they are and the personal biographies they bring to the workplace.

When Concerns Are the Concern

Kelly entered college knowing she wanted to teach middle school. She loved to write and read, so language arts seemed like a natural. Five years later, she had her own classroom and was navigating her way through her first year of teaching with the support of her mentor, Fran. An experienced mentor teacher, Fran had been recruited to participate in a video program that I was producing on the lives of first-year teachers. As we worked together on the project, Fran took the opportunity to tell me about her current mentee, whom she described as incredibly needy. "I don't think I have ever met someone who needed more affirmation. She needs to develop a thicker skin or something. She worries about what people say, what they don't say, how they look at her, if they don't look at her. It's so sad to see someone that fragile." When I asked Fran how Kelly was performing in the classroom, she explained that: "She is doing fine for a first-year teacher. Like everyone, she has good days and bad. The difference is she seems to doubt herself even on the good days." When I asked how she was dealing with this, Fran explained that she was growing weary of having to constantly worry about Kelly's state of mind. "I am afraid I lost my patience last week. She asked me if I thought the principal respected her and I told her she needed to quit worrying about whether other people respected her, and learn to start respecting herself."

Fuller's (1969) Stages of Concern Theory continues to drive research and theorizing on teacher development. This theory, which proposes that teachers experience three developmental stages throughout their careers, may have been a helpful way for Fran to put Kelly's needs into perspective, perhaps leading to deeper understanding and acceptance. Kelly's strong desire for affirmation and her apparent fear of rejection by others are indicators of the "Survival Stage" of teaching, in which beginning teachers tend to be most concerned about issues related to "self." Such issues often take the form of questions, such as: Will I be accepted? Am I capable of meeting the expectations of others? Did I make the right career choice? Will I make it in this school? Such concerns are not unrelated to those found near the bottom of Maslow's (1943) hierarchy of needs, which he described as love, belongingness, and acceptance needs.

Although almost all beginning teachers experience survival concerns, their intensity and duration vary from individual to individual. The ways in which such concerns manifest themselves also vary. For example, while Fran no doubt had mentored beginning teachers in the past who were in the Survival Stage, she had not experienced someone for whom the concerns were so strong, and so overtly expressed. By the way, it is important to realize that Fuller's (1969) Stages of Concern Theory is not a chronological age theory. Veteran teachers may well return to this stage at any age—and at any point in their careers—if their primary concerns, for whatever reasons, become once again focused on issues of self. It is also important to understand that one cannot skip or leapfrog over the various stages. Beginning teachers start in the Survival Stage and then work their way through the Task Stage, hopefully arriving at the Impact Stage of teaching. How quickly one moves from stage to stage, or how long one is arrested at a particular stage, is a function of many forces. What is important for mentors to appreciate is that theoretically one cannot move from one stage to another until the concerns of the earlier stage have been satisfied. With this understanding in mind, high-performance mentors carefully observe their mentees, listening for personal expressions of concern and looking for behaviors that might suggest that they are dealing with issues associated with a particular stage.

Finally, once they develop a personal theory about which stage their beginning teacher is in, high-performance mentors employ mentoring behaviors aimed at helping them meet the concerns associated with that stage. For example, Fran might have selected one or more of the following mentor behaviors in her effort to help Kelly satisfy her survival concerns:

1. Look for opportunities to provide specific praise of some particular aspect of the mentee's professional practice.

2. Express personal interest in the mentee's professional ideas.

3. Facilitate the mentee to reflect on things that are going well and encourage him or her to celebrate their successes.

4. Invite the mentee to social or professional activities.

5. Share one's own survival stories, emphasizing the preoccupation you felt with being accepted and approved.

6. Look for opportunities to compliment the mentee in public settings where other teachers, administrators, or parents are present.

After working through the issues associated with the Survival Stage, beginning teachers typically focus their concerns on issues related to the Task Stage of teaching. In this second developmental stage, teachers are primarily concerned with issues of time and task. Such concerns are commonly associated with a focus on improving one's classroom management strategies, finding or developing instructional materials, or finding more efficient ways to manage other duties and school-related responsibilities. Teachers in this stage tend to ask themselves questions such as: How can I improve this test? Where can I find a better piece of literature for this unit? How can I reorganize my classroom to make it run more smoothly? How can I do all that is expected of me? With Fran's acceptance and encouragement, Kelly will eventually shift her preoccupation with self-focused issues to these more technical and professional concerns. When that occurs, Fran will face the new challenge of helping Kelly deal effectively with her new concerns. In doing so, she may find one or more of the following mentoring strategies to be helpful:

1. Help the mentee prioritize the many tasks that he or she feels compelled to complete.

2. Provide instructional resources, including lesson plans or instructional materials that can help the mentee save time.

3. Share your personal methods for efficiently accomplishing instructional, student assessment, or classroom management tasks.

4. Help connect the mentee with colleagues who have expertise in the areas the mentee has expressed interest in improving.

5. Encourage the mentee to reflect on the motive he or she may have for pursuing a particular task.

6. Help the mentee develop a time- and task-management system.

The third and final stage in Fuller's (1969) Concerns Theory is the Impact Stage. At this stage, teachers' primary and driving concerns are with students and their learning. Such concerns focus on ensuring that learning experiences are meaningful and appropriate to the needs of students. Teachers at this stage also exhibit a generalized concern for the well-being of students with a focus on preparing them for their continuing education and for life beyond school. Typical questions from impact-level teachers might include: Are students learning this material? Have they acquired the knowledge, skills, and dispositions for future success in school?

One of Fran's goals as a high-performance mentor should be to help Kelly become an Impact Stage teacher. She cannot do this by telling her that it is important, or by constantly reminding her that she should be focused on students. What she can do is help Kelly satisfy her survival- and task-related concerns, allowing her to eventually come to that place where impact concerns drive her daily practice. Accepting Kelly and her survival concerns is Fran's first step in this important process. Hopefully, she will eventually have the opportunity to support Kelly as she shifts her primary concerns to students and their learning. When that occurs, Fran may find the following mentoring behaviors to be helpful:

1. Commend the mentee for being student-centered.

2. Engage the mentee in collegial dialogue focused on meeting the needs of individual learners.

3. Introduce the mentee to more complex teaching models and strategies.

4. Encourage the mentee to collaborate with or observe exemplary teachers who model best practices that the beginning teacher has not incorporated in his or her own classroom.

5. Focus dialogue on the mentee's efforts to meet the needs of his most challenging students.

6. Help the mentee develop improved methods for assessing student learning.

When reading the above recommendations for helping the beginning teacher who is transitioning to the Impact Stage, there may be a tendency to feel as if such strategies cannot wait, that they are too important and should be emphasized early in the mentoring relationship. This feeling is understandable. To clarify, there is nothing to prevent a mentor from employing such strategies early in a mentoring relationship. Whether they will make the kind of impact that the mentor hopes will depend on where the beginning teacher is in terms of his or her own concerns. In many ways, this reality is not unlike the one experienced by teachers in their interactions with students. The very best teachers understand that helping students engage in more challenging material is a function not only of holding high expectations, but of creating the interpersonal context that meets the needs and interests of those students.

Several years ago, I was facilitating a mentor teacher workshop and had just finished explaining Fuller's (1969) Stages of Concern Theory when a veteran teacher volunteered that she had found the theory quite interesting, and that it had caused her to reflect on her own journey through the stages. She went on to describe how she clearly remembered a specific day from her first year of teaching. "It was February 13, 1969, probably about 7:30 in the evening." The date and time were so precise because she remembered leaving school after finishing her plans for the next day. As she walked down the halls of the empty school, she realized that the next day was Valentine's Day. Suddenly, she was confronted by the fact that every classroom in her third- and fourth-grade hallway was decorated with hearts and cupids of varied design.

"I couldn't believe that I had somehow been so isolated as to miss what was going on around me. On the other hand," she added, "I wasn't in a relationship with anyone, as school life had pretty much consumed my personal life." She then described how she turned around, returned to her room, and spent the next 2 hours decorating her classroom while in tears. "I can now see why I went back. I didn't want the children to think that I didn't care about them, and I didn't want the other teachers or the principal to think I was out of touch with the world. I went back to meet my survival concerns." She then went on to quickly finish her story. "The next year was so much better. I marked the day on my calendar, and the students cut out the hearts and helped decorate the room. My room was one of the first and best decorated. I guess I had moved on to the Task Stage." Finally, she said, "Today, I don't worry so much about whether the room is decorated, although it usually is. For the last few years, my biggest concern has been making sure that each Valentine's Day I engage my students in a lesson about love."

Challenge, Skill, and Flow

Charlie was a veteran special educator assigned to mentor a first-year intervention specialist in an urban junior high school. Brandy was 24 years old and had just completed her 5-year program at a state university, graduating with her master's in special education. Charlie was excited to have a new teacher in his department, especially one with Brandy's credentials. In recent years, he had been asked to mentor a number of first-year teachers who were hired in special education positions despite having no formal training in the field. I met Charlie when he enrolled in one of my evening graduate classes at the university. After a class in which we had spent some time talking about mentoring, Charlie hung around to talk about a recent experience he had with his mentee. Quickly it became apparent that he had had some strong feelings, not only about Brandy but about her university training as well. "I've got this new teacher, with a master's degree, in special ed no less. And guess what? She's asking me questions about writing IEPs [Individualized Educational Plans]. I spent 2 hours last week teaching her how to write measurable goals and how to prepare a transition plan." Before I could ask him if he felt that was something he should be doing as a mentor, Charlie interrupted: "Come on, that's not my job. That's a fundamental skill she should have mastered in school. Isn't that what a master's degree means?"

There are two important perspectives that may have helped Charlie better understand Brandy's need for help. The first has to do with Charlie's conception of his role as a mentor teacher. It would be very helpful if he believed that it was his job to help Brandy develop her professional skills. High-performance mentors understand that most professional skills are developed through practice. In fields such as medicine, law, engineering, and many others, skill development occurs under the guidance of veteran practitioners who assume responsibility for helping novices develop and refine their skills through extended internship experiences. High-performance mentors see the early years of teaching as a time of skill development and commit themselves to helping beginning teachers through this important period. Low-performance mentors, by contrast, tend to believe that beginning teachers should arrive on the job fully prepared, and for them "fully prepared" means highly skilled. They are often disappointed and blame the mentee or the mentee's college for their "poor preparation."

Charlie might have been more understanding of Brandy's needs if he had considered them in light of Flow Theory as advanced by Csikszentmihalyi (1977, 1997). In this intriguing theory, which is now garnering attention from educators, people find themselves in "flow" when they are deeply and effortlessly involved in tasks that they have a good chance of successfully completing. Such a state is also characterized by a sense of clear goals and the opportunity for immediate feedback.

At the foundation of Flow Theory is the idea that being in flow is a function of the degree of "skill" one brings to an activity or task, and the degree of "challenge" one experiences in the process of performance (See Figure 4.1).

When there is a balance between skill and challenge, flow is more likely to occur, and people become deeply engaged to the extent that time can seem to be suspended. However, if one's skill is low and the challenge high, flow is replaced by a sense of anxiety and a preoccupation with the difficulty of the task, and the potential for failure. In contrast, if one's skill

Figure 4.1   Flow as a Function of Skill and Challenge

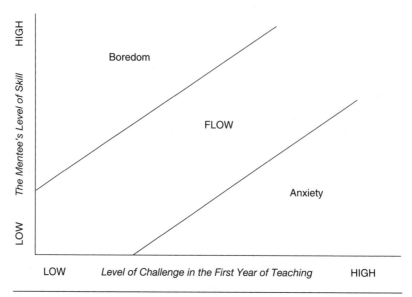

SOURCE: Adapted from Csikszentmihalyi (1977).

is high and the challenge low, boredom replaces flow (See Figure 4.2).

After introducing Flow Theory to mentors-in-training, I ask them where they would plot beginning teachers on the skill axis of the flow graph. "Are their skills typically low, moderate, or high?" I ask. Although the opinions are mixed, most believe they tend to be moderate. In some respects, the question is an unfair one because it requires a generalization about beginning teachers. The reality is that skill levels not only differ by individual, but are context-specific to the challenge encountered as well. One beginning teacher has low skill in managing student behavior, but moderate skill in planning instruction, whereas another has high behavior-management skill, and low skill in planning. What new and experienced mentors agree on is that the challenges encountered in the first year tend to be high. Again, what is important to remember is that challenge is personal and context-specific as well.

Filling out 20 or more "real" IEPs, for the first time, in the context of a new school environment, is likely going to be

Figure 4.2   Boredom and Anxiety

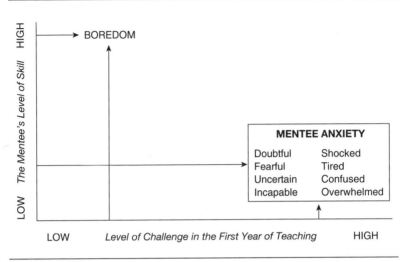

SOURCE: Adapted from Csikszentmihalyi (1977).

a high-challenge task for many beginning teachers, and Brandy was no exception. Although she had good knowledge of the IEP process and some clinical experience in her university preparation, her skill level was still relatively low. The high anxiety Brandy manifested, and which Charlie was having difficulty accepting, was predictable and understandable from a Flow Theory perspective.

Commitment and Cognition

A mentor teacher named Sharon described what she called her "mixed feelings" about her mentee when participating in a mentor teacher panel I had organized for a mentoring workshop. I had recruited experienced mentors from a district several miles away so that the mentors-in-training could ask questions, and the panelists could respond with less concern that someone in the audience might know the beginning teacher who was being mentored.

Sharon was a high school music teacher and band director assigned to mentor a beginning music teacher named Tom, who was hired to be the assistant band director as well. "What is so interesting to me," Sharon began "is how hard he tries, but how many things he seems to miss." Sharon had the luxury of being able to work closely with Tom on an almost daily basis, as the two of them shared responsibility for planning and leading band practice. Sharon went on to describe how Tom was highly committed to the music program and to the students. "He's not afraid of work. That's for sure. He volunteers to help in all kinds of ways, and always follows through." When I asked what she meant about having mixed emotions, she explained that Tom didn't seem to be able to hear or see some of the mistakes that students were making in their performances. "It's frustrating because we will both hear the same performance. When I ask him what he thinks, I am often surprised by the things he seems to miss. I find myself trying to solve problems he doesn't think exist."

Accepting beginning teachers can also be enhanced when mentor teachers strive to understand them in terms of their developmental level. One way of thinking about developmental level has been advanced by Glickman (2002), who suggests that developmental level can be viewed as a function of two important factors, "commitment" and level of "abstract thinking." The next chapter provides an in-depth treatment of Glickman's (2002) theory and an explanation of these two important constructs. For now, it will suffice to say that beginning teachers show up on the job with varying levels of both commitment and abstract thinking ability. From Sharon's brief descriptions of Tom, it appears that he is high on the commitment continuum and perhaps low to moderate in his level of abstraction. This is not good, bad, normal, or abnormal. It is where Tom is at this point in his career, and where Sharon needs to meet him with acceptance and understanding.

ACCEPTANCE INDICATORS

The High-Performance Mentoring Framework includes five indicators related to acceptance. Reviewing these indicators periodically can provide mentors with the opportunity to reflect on the extent to which they have accepted the person they are seeking to help. The five indicators for *Accepts the Beginning Teacher as a Developing Person and Professional* are:

1. Values acceptance as the foundation of a helping relationship

2. Understands the differences among beginning teachers from multiple perspectives

3. Endeavors to see the world through the mentee's eyes

4. Communicates respect and positive regard for the mentee

5. Models acceptance of diversity in others

Values Acceptance

An important part of the process of becoming a high-performance mentor is becoming a more accepting person. This process begins with an awareness of acceptance and its relationship to mentoring, but awareness is not enough. In order to advance the process, one must truly value the critically important role that acceptance plays in promoting the growth and development of those we seek to help. Only then are we likely to begin to monitor and manage our personal judgments, and begin to seek the understandings that eventually lead to authentic acceptance. This journey is not an easy one, but those mentors who commit themselves to the process increase the odds that they will make a meaningful impact on the lives of those they seek to help.

Understanding Differences

Understanding and acceptance are complementary constructs. One informs the other. Mentors who understand that beginning teachers are different and alike, and can think about those differences from multiple perspectives, are likely to be more accepting. In reverse, mentors who are accepting of beginning teachers are more likely to open themselves to deeper understanding. There are many ways to try to more fully understand the experience of being a first-year teacher. In this chapter, I have introduced five such methods, each of which is worthy of deeper exploration by mentors committed to expanding their ways of thinking about the lives of those they seek to help.

Seeing the World Through Their Eyes

One of the benefits of reading about the problems and concerns of beginning teachers is that it provides mentors with the opportunity to reflect on their own first-year experiences, increasing the chance that they may be able to set their own values aside temporarily, and view the world through the eyes of their mentee. When a beginning teacher approaches a mentor with a particular problem or concern, it is quite normal for the mentor to begin processing the issue from his or her veteran perspective. This can be both good and bad, depending on what transpires. First, it is good because veteran perspectives are valuable. When thoughtfully shared, they can be very helpful. However, it can be bad if the mentor is not aware that his or her perspective may well not be the perspective held by the beginning teacher. In the best interactions, mentees sense that the mentor sees, knows, or feels the problem from the mentee's point of view. This acknowledgment makes them more open to continued reflection and conversation. In the worst interactions, mentees quickly conclude that their perspective has not been heard, understood, or accepted and they begin to become defensive, or decide to seek help elsewhere.

Communicating Respect and Positive Regard

It is easy to communicate respect and positive regard to someone we like, or someone with beliefs, values, and behaviors similar to our own. It is not so easy to do so with someone whom we may not like, or who is quite different from ourselves. Acceptance and understanding, however, make it possible for mentors to communicate respect and positive regard even in these more challenging situations. In fact, high-performance mentors recognize the special importance of doing so in precisely these situations. When we authentically communicate respect and positive regard, we take a giant step toward creating the conditions in which a helpful relationship can develop. When we fail to do so, the odds of facilitating growth and development in the other begin to stack against us.

Models Acceptance of Others

High-performance mentors understand that they can be role models as well as mentors. They are aware that they may teach as much by their daily words and actions with students, parents, and colleagues as they do by their personal interactions with the beginning teacher. Consequently, they endeavor to take the high road rather than the lower one, which is far more tempting to travel.

QUESTIONS FOR REFLECTION ON ACCEPTING

- Have you accepted your beginning teacher? Or, are you in a state of judgment with regard to his or her thoughts and behaviors?
- Do you agree with Rogers's (1961) claim that acceptance is "a highly important element in a helping relationship" (p. 34)? Or, do you believe that it is unnecessary as long as you have good advice to give, good ideas to share?
- Have you experienced defensiveness on the part of your mentee? If so, have you reflected on the possibility that your mentee may have sensed a lack of acceptance?
- Can you accept yourself, when you find yourself failing to accept another?

- Are you willing to understand and accept the problems experienced by your mentee as predictable yet idiosyncratic?
- Are you willing to understand and accept that beginning teachers react differently to the socializing forces of school?
- Are you willing to understand and accept that beginning teachers have developmental levels of concern that vary in intensity, duration, and in the manner in which they are manifested?
- Are you willing to understand and accept that beginning teachers are often out of flow and in a state of anxiety because their skill levels do not match the challenges they are encountering?
- Are you willing to understand and accept that beginning teachers vary with regard to their levels of commitment and their abilities to think abstractly about various aspects of their practice?
- Have you committed to trying to become the observer of your own thoughts and behaviors, especially with regard to monitoring your tendency to judge rather than accept?

5

Communicating

*The greatest problem in communication is the illusion
that it has been accomplished.*

—George Bernard Shaw

*The most important thing in communication is to hear
what isn't being said.*

—Peter Drucker

*To effectively communicate, we must realize that we are
all different in the way we perceive the world and use
this understanding as a guide to our communication
with others.*

—Anthony Robbins

If a good mentoring relationship is like a good conversation,
then the high-performance mentor must be a good con-
versationalist. Effective interpersonal communication is a
complex phenomenon that can be examined from a number
of different perspectives. For example, there is a good chance
that as an educator you have attended workshops on active
listening, nonverbal communication, or perhaps even neural
linguistic programming. These three aspects of communication are directly tied to the three quotes at the beginning of

this chapter. By using active listening skills aimed at checking to see if a message has been accurately sent or received, one can work against the problem that George Bernard Shaw described as *the illusion of understanding*. By attending to the nonverbal messages that characterize any conversation, one can, as Peter Drucker suggests, begin to *hear what isn't being said*. Finally, by heightening our awareness of how others perceive the world, we can *program our conversational behaviors* to be more congruent with those of the person we are seeking to help. These are but three aspects of effective interpersonal communication. Much has been written about each that is worthy of study by mentor teachers intent on improving their communication skills.

All of us have been in good conversations—and in bad ones as well. Both are memorable, or perhaps unforgettable, for different reasons. Before introducing a theoretical perspective on communication that is especially relevant to the work of the high-performance mentor, allow me to revisit a personal experience with a conversation that, for me, fits into the unforgettable category. Later, we will revisit the story from a theoretical perspective

A CONVERSATION REVISITED

A few years ago, my friend Scott and I decided to take up the sport of fly fishing. Several hundred dollars' worth of equipment later, we made a couple of unsuccessful forays to the Smoky Mountains, only to realize that we needed some coaching. After some discussion we decided to make another trip, this time hiring a guide for the day. In preparation for our guided trip, we read a couple of books, watched a video on fly-fishing techniques, and even took a one-day "Fly-Fishing Basics" class at the local YMCA.

We met Allen for breakfast in a small-town restaurant in North Carolina to begin our day. He explained what streams we would fish, what species of trout we would be after, and how he planned to teach us the basics of fly fishing. Over breakfast, we listened as Allen shared his personal history as a fly fisherman. This included detailed descriptions of specific trout he had caught on three different continents, the type of fly he used in each case, and the difficult presentation he had to make to hook each one. When he asked the waitress to bring another pot of coffee to our table, Scott and I exchanged concerned glances, wondering whether we would ever get our waders on that day.

Eventually, we made it to the stream, where Allen spent about an hour demonstrating different casting techniques. We watched as he made effortless and accurate casts while explaining the necessary techniques. After watching and listening, and none too soon for us, Allen turned us loose to "work the stream." Scott went one way and I the other, both happy to have the opportunity to experiment with what we had learned and naively anxious to hook our first trout. It was almost 11 A.M. when we began to wade away from Allen's truck, which was parked by the side of the stream. "Let's meet back here at noon for lunch and we can have a little conversation about flies." Walking in opposite directions, one upstream and one down, Scott and I turned immediately and made eye contact. From a hundred feet apart we exchanged the same glance that we had across the table at breakfast. Both of us knew there would be no *conversation* about flies, and we were right.

Allen was extremely knowledgeable about entomology, which he was studying at the University of North Carolina before he decided to pursue fly fishing full-time. After about 40 minutes of listening to him describe more than 20 different flies and the actual insects they were designed to imitate, using their formal Latin names, I decided to run an experiment to see if he could read nonverbal messages. I sat down, leaned against a tree, and began sharpening my pocketknife. Five minutes later, he was still describing flies as if I were hanging on his every word.

Eventually, I felt guilty for leaving Scott in the awkward position of having to feign interest, and eventually rejoined him for Allen's demonstration of the stomach pump, and how it could be used to extract half-digested flies from the belly of a trout, enabling the fisherman to accurately "match the hatch."

Don't get me wrong; Allen was very knowledgeable. He no doubt was an expert at matching flies on a trout stream. Unfortunately, with regard to interpersonal communication, he failed to match his presentation to our developmental needs. We were novice fly fishermen, full of excitement and anticipation. Yes, we needed technical assistance. No doubt we needed baseline information. But mostly we needed to have an initial success. Ideally, that would have meant catching a trout, which we did not. However, being on the stream would have been enough, especially if we had felt welcomed and respected for our personal histories of fishing and outdoor adventuring. We tried to tell him about our many years of guiding canoe trips in Canada and how we hoped to fly fish for smallmouth bass on our next trip. Not once did he bite on any of our conversational lures. At the end of the day, he gave us a pitch about coming back for another day of advanced instruction. He also encouraged us to consider signing up for one of his guided trips to Montana.

DEVELOPMENTAL MENTORING

Needless to say, there would be no day two, much less a 2-week expedition to Big Sky Country. Scott and I picked up a couple of good ideas from Allen, but had no desire to continue our relationship. Saying good-bye after he dropped us off at our car was our last communication. Again, I want to make clear that there were many things that Scott and I could have learned from Allen. Unfortunately, he did not establish the conversational rapport that would have allowed him to have an ongoing impact. Such can be the case with knowledgeable and even well-intentioned mentors who fail the test of good conversation.

The purpose of this chapter is to focus on one specific aspect of communication that is critical to maintaining quality conversations between mentors and beginning teachers. It represents a specific way of thinking about effective communication in the context of the mentoring relationship. This particular approach, which I call *developmental mentoring,* is based on the writings of Glickman (1985) and his theory of *developmental supervision.* I realize that *supervision* is a word that most mentor teachers do not associate with the mentoring process. Nonetheless, I am convinced that a deeper understanding of this theory can powerfully influence a mentor teacher's ability to be a more thoughtful and effective communicator. If Allen had understood this theory, he may well have earned some repeat business, and Scott and I might have more quickly developed our fly-fishing knowledge and skill.

BELIEFS INFLUENCE PRACTICE

One of the basic tenets of the developmental approach to mentoring is that one's beliefs about mentoring tend to influence the ways in which one prefers to communicate with beginning teachers. Because of this claim, it is important that you have the opportunity to better understand your personal beliefs before I provide a fuller explanation of the theory, and how it can support your efforts to become a high-performance mentor. The Mentor Beliefs Inventory is a 15-item, forced-choice instrument that was adapted from Glickman's Supervisor Beliefs Inventory (1985). There are no right or wrong answers to the questions, as the goal of the instrument is simply to help you gain insight into your personal beliefs about mentoring and how those beliefs may influence your mentoring behaviors. If you are currently working with a first-year teacher, you may want to think about that teacher whenever an item refers to beginning teachers. If you have mentored in the past, but currently are not assigned to a beginning teacher, you may choose to think of a teacher you have mentored in previous years. If you are new to mentoring, you will want to think about each item in more general terms. After taking the inventory, you may self-score your responses by using the scoring guide that follows.

THE MENTOR TEACHER BELIEFS INVENTORY

This inventory is designed for mentor teachers to assess their own beliefs about mentoring and professional development. The inventory assumes that mentor teachers believe and act according to three theoretical orientations to mentoring, but that one usually dominates. The inventory is designed to be self-administered and self-scored. Mentor teachers are asked to choose one of the two options. A scoring guide follows. See Figure 5.1.

Instructions: Circle either A or B for each item. If you do not completely agree with either choice, choose the one that is closer to how you feel.

1. A. Mentor teachers should give beginning teachers a large degree of autonomy and initiative within broadly defined limits.
   B. Mentor teachers should give beginning teachers directions about methods that will help them improve their teaching.

2. A. It is important for beginning teachers to set their own goals and objectives for professional growth.
   B. It is important for mentor teachers to help beginning teachers reconcile their personalities and teaching styles with the philosophy and direction of the school.

3. A. Beginning teachers are likely to feel uncomfortable and anxious if their mentors do not tell them what they will be focusing on during classroom observations.
   B. Classroom observations of beginning teachers are meaningless if beginning teachers are not able to define with their mentor teachers the focus or foci of the observation.

4. A. An open, trusting, warm, and personal relationship with beginning teachers is the most important ingredient in mentoring beginning teachers.
   B. Mentor teachers who are too personal with beginning teachers risk being less effective and less respected than mentors who keep a certain degree of professional distance from beginning teachers.

5. A. My role during mentoring conferences is to make the interaction positive, to share realistic information, and to help beginning teachers plan their own solutions to problems.
   B. The methods and strategies I use with beginning teachers in a conference are aimed at our reaching agreement over the needs for future improvement.

6. In the initial phase of working with a beginning teacher:
   A. I develop objectives with the teacher(s) that will help accomplish school goals.
   B. I try to identify the talents and goals of the individual beginning teachers so they can work on their own improvement.

7. When several teachers in a building have a similar classroom problem, I prefer to:
   A. Have beginning teachers form an ad hoc group to help them work together to solve the problem.
   B. Help beginning teachers on an individual basis find their strengths, abilities, and resources so that each one finds his or her own solution to the problem.

8. The most important clue that an entry-year workshop is needed occurs when:
   A. A mentor perceives that several beginning teachers lack knowledge or skill in a specific area, which is resulting in low morale, undue stress, and less effective teaching.
   B. Several beginning teachers perceive the need to strengthen their abilities in the same instructional area.

(Continued)

(Continued)

9. A. Practicing mentors should decide the objectives of any entry-year workshops, because they have a broad perspective on beginning teachers' abilities and the school's needs.
   B. Mentor teachers and beginning teachers should reach consensus about the objectives of any entry-year workshop.

10. A. Beginning teachers who feel they are growing personally will be more effective than beginning teachers who are not experiencing personal growth.
    B. Beginning teachers should employ teaching methods that have proven successful over the years.

11. When I observe a beginning teacher scolding a student unnecessarily:
    A. I explain, during a post-observation conference with the teacher, why the scolding was excessive.
    B. I ask the teacher about the incident, but do not interject my judgments.

12. A. One effective way to improve beginning teacher performance is for mentors to formulate clear professional improvement plans for beginning teachers.
    B. Professional development plans are helpful to some beginning teachers but stifling to others.

13. During a pre-observation conference:
    A. I suggest to the teacher what I could observe, but I let the teacher make the final decision about the objectives and methods of observation.
    B. The teacher and I mutually decide the objectives and methods of observation.

14. A. Improvement occurs very slowly if beginning teachers are left on their own, but when a group of beginning teachers and their mentors works together on a specific problem, they learn rapidly and their morale remains high.

> B. Group activities may be enjoyable, but I find that providing individual guidance to a beginning teacher leads to more sustained results.
>
> 15. When an entry-year program meeting is scheduled:
>   A. All mentor teachers who participated in the decision to hold the meeting should be expected to attend it.
>   B. Mentor teachers, regardless of their role in calling for or planning the meeting, should be able to decide if the workshop is relevant to their personal or professional growth and, if not, should not be expected to attend.

Interpreting Your Scores

Before proceeding with an explanation of your scores from the inventory, you will want to make sure that you calculated accurately. One good way to check is to add your final three scores. They should total 100, give or take a fraction of a point. If your total is off by more than that, you have a math error that you will want to find and correct. Your final three scores represent the approximate percentage of time you are likely to employ each of three approaches to mentoring. Specifically, your 2.1 score is your *directive* score. Your 2.2 score is your *collaborative* score, and 2.3 is your *nondirective* score. Most likely, you have scores in all three areas. It is possible, however, that you may have a zero in one area. It is also possible that your scores in two areas might be very close or identical. What is important to understand is that your highest score represents your preferred approach. If, for example, your highest score is 60.3 in the collaborative area, you theoretically would be expected to employ such an approach about 60 percent of the time when working with a beginning teacher. In contrast, if

Figure 5.1   Developmental Mentoring Scoring Guide

Step 1. Circle your answers to the inventory in the following columns:

Column I	Column II	Column III
1B	1A	
	2B	2A
3A		3B
4B		4A
	5B	5A
6A		6B
	7A	7B
8A		8B
9A	9B	
10B		10A
11A		11B
12A	12B	
	13B	13A
14B	14A	
15A	15B	

Step 2. Tally the number of circled items in each column and multiply by 6.7.

2.1. Total responses in Column I _____ 6.7 = _____
2.2. Total responses in Column II _____ 6.7 = _____
2.3. Total responses in Column III _____ 6.7 = _____

Step 3. Interpretation: Refer to the following page to gain insight into your scores.

your directive score was 6.7, you would be expected to use such an approach only about 7 percent of the time. Your next challenge is to reflect on your scores by asking whether you believe they have *face validity*. Face validity refers to your personal assessment of whether the scores seem to be an accurate representation of who you are and how you prefer to interact with beginning teachers in a mentoring relationship. The following brief explanations of the three approaches should help you with this process.

Directive Approach

Mentor teachers with high directive scores may tend to believe that beginning teachers are best served when their mentors provide professional advice and guidance that is grounded in the mentor's knowledge and experience. Consequently, such mentors may feel most comfortable when providing strategic or technical advice. If you are, or could imagine yourself being, most comfortable telling a beginning teacher what to do, or how to do it, you may tend to prefer the directive approach. Clearly, this was Allen's preferred approach to guiding novice fly fishers.

Collaborative Approach

Mentor teachers who take a predominantly collaborative approach to mentoring may tend to believe that beginning teachers benefit most when their mentors relate to them in more interactive ways. Consequently, mentors with a preference for this approach may feel most comfortable when engaged in collegial dialogue or collaborative problem solving. If you are, or could imagine yourself being, most comfortable exchanging ideas with a beginning teacher or working together on an instructional unit, you most likely prefer the collaborative approach to mentoring. This is the approach that Scott and I would have preferred, and felt we deserved.

Nondirective Approach

Mentor teachers who prefer a nondirective mentoring style may tend to believe that beginning teachers profit most when their mentors provide them with the professional autonomy to find their own way, and solve their own problems. Such mentors may feel most comfortable when listening to or encouraging beginning teachers. If you are, or could imagine yourself being, most comfortable listening to the ideas of a beginning teacher while facilitating his or her thinking by asking clarifying questions, you most likely prefer a nondirective approach to mentoring. This approach would not have been appropriate for Scott and me, because we did not have enough experience to be truly self-directed.

Consequently, no one approach is judged to be superior to another. All three approaches have value when they are thoughtfully employed. Therefore, whereas there is no *best* set of scores on the inventory, one might argue that there is a *theoretically ideal* set of scores. A mentor with equal scores in all three approaches may be best equipped to employ whatever approach is most appropriate for his or her beginning teacher. It is important here to point out that your scores can, and likely will, change with time and experience. They are not calcified personality traits that lock you into only one way of thinking or behaving. This is especially true if you are willing to experiment with new communication behaviors that lie outside your comfort zone. For example, the first time I took the Supervisor Beliefs Inventory (Glickman, 1985) I scored a zero in the directive area. After reflecting on that score, I acknowledged that it had face validity for me because I definitely was not comfortable directing other adults. Several years later, after supervising student teachers, I took the inventory again, only to discover that my directive score had gone from 0 to 33.5.

Now that you have a basic understanding of the three approaches, it is time to address the other important concept that lies at the heart of developmental mentoring. That concept can be summarized as follows: High-performance mentors are aware of the three approaches and strategically employ communication behaviors from the approach that best matches the developmental level of the beginning teacher they are seeking to help.

Identifying Developmental Level

There are many ways to think about the developmental level of beginning teachers, but for our purposes we will be primarily concerned with two specific factors identified by Glickman (2002): level of *commitment* and level of *abstract thinking*.

Level of Commitment

Picture, if you will, a continuum of commitment ranging from low to high. At the low end, one would find beginning teachers who manifest patterns of behavior that indicate little or no genuine commitment to teaching. This may take the form of a lack of concern for students, lack of time and energy devoted to critical professional tasks, and an overriding concern with one's personal issues or job security. At the opposite end, you would find beginning teachers who demonstrate a high degree of concern for students as well as fellow teachers. These individuals evidence this concern by dedicating the time and energy necessary to meet the needs of students. They are concerned with doing a good job, not only to secure their position, but also because they feel a sense of obligation to those they serve and work with on a daily basis. Obviously, beginning teachers do not always fall to either end of the commitment continuum. Instead, they are distributed along the continuum in three general levels: low, moderate, and high.

Level of Abstract Thinking

Now, in similar fashion, picture a continuum of abstract thinking that also ranges from low to high. At the low end of abstract thinking, beginning teachers are unaware of the problems they are having, or are confused about the nature of the problem, lacking the ability, for example, to clearly define the problem. Such teachers typically lack the wherewithal to develop possible solutions and may believe that there is a correct or right method. In such cases, their preference is for someone to tell them what to do. At the opposite and high end of abstract thinking, beginning teachers have the capacity to analyze professional dilemmas from multiple perspectives, are capable of crafting alternative solutions, and have the personal efficacy to make a decision and see it through.

Again, at the heart of developmental mentoring is an understanding that mentors must be thoughtful observers of beginning teachers, for the purpose of establishing a general sense of their developmental level with regard to commitment and abstract thinking. In a sense, this involves the process of informal assessment. One gains insight through conversation and observation over time, and then selects communication behaviors designed to meet the needs of the mentee and eventually support him or her in moving to higher levels of commitment and abstraction.

Matching Mentoring Communications to Developmental Level

Now that you have a fundamental understanding of the three approaches to mentoring and the concept of developmental level, you are ready to put the theory into practice. Each of the three approaches to mentoring—nondirective, collaborative, and directive—can be associated with different types of communication behaviors. See Figure 5.2.

For example, you will notice that sample nondirective behaviors include listening, clarifying, and encouraging. These are appropriate communication skills to employ when the mentor senses that the beginning teacher is developmentally high and capable of thinking through her problems, or when there is little question that the mentee is highly committed to taking whatever actions are necessary to deal with the problem

Figure 5.2   The Mentoring Behavior Continuum

Nondirective Mentoring Behaviors	Collaborative Mentoring Behaviors	Directive Mentoring Behaviors
Listening	Reflecting	Directing
Clarifying	Presenting	Standardizing
Encouraging	Problem Solving	Reinforcing
	Negotiating	

Mentee's *Developmental Level* as a function of:

High   ←——————   *Commitment*   ——————→   Low
High   ←——————   *Abstract Thinking*   ——————→   Low

SOURCE: Adapted from Glickman (1985).

at hand. Such approaches work well because they affirm the beginning teacher's sense of being a capable professional with the capacity to be an independent problem solver. Imagine the beginning teacher who, in a post-observation conference, is asked by her mentor if there are any things that she might want to change the next time she teaches this material. The developmentally high teacher will likely provide a thoughtful response that includes specific ideas for how things might be improved. The thoughtful mentor, recognizing the high levels of commitment and abstraction being evidenced, is content with nondirective responses, feeling no personal need to interject his or her own opinions into the conversation.

Communication behaviors such as reflecting, presenting, problem solving, and negotiating represent collaborative behaviors that mentors can employ when they believe a beginning teacher is at a moderate developmental level and can profit most from dialogue and the exchange of ideas. Such approaches are most helpful to beginning teachers who may need some support in conceptualizing a problem or potential problem, or in crafting appropriate solutions. Such approaches are also appropriate when beginning teachers are somewhat committed, but perhaps need additional assurance. Imagine the first-year science teacher who finds himself in the middle of a classroom debate about evolution and creation theory. He is caught off guard by the intensity of the debate and the fact that a couple of students resorted to shouting and name-calling. Unsure of what to do the next day in class, he decides to speak with his mentor. The mentor takes a collaborative approach, recognizing that his mentee sees parts of the problem and is committed to taking action, but is unaware of other important dimensions of the problem that need to be addressed. They work together to negotiate a plan for how to deal with the issue the next day, and agree to meet after school to discuss how things played out in practice.

Finally, there are the behaviors of directing, standardizing, and reinforcing. Such approaches are most appropriate when the mentor recognizes that the beginning teacher is operating at a relatively low developmental level. Such approaches are particularly important when the mentor believes that the beginning teacher is behaving in a way that ultimately will be self-defeating. Imagine the beginning teacher who prides herself on her "adventurous approach" to teaching. Believing in not missing the teachable moment, she takes her fourth graders on a spontaneous field trip into the neighborhood surrounding the school. Teachers in her hallway report the event to the mentor, asking her to address the problem. After some reflection, the mentor decides to bring up the incident in her next meeting with the mentee. Unfortunately, when she does, things do not go well. When the beginning teacher becomes defensive, arguing that her creativity is being stifled and that she has no plans to discontinue the practice, the mentor clearly expresses her concern, directing the mentee to continue thinking creatively, but not to leave the building without informing the office.

FROM THEORY TO PRACTICE

A few years ago, I was conducting a mentor teacher support session in the school district where I once taught. All the mentors had previous mentoring experience and were currently working with a formally assigned beginning teacher. The purpose of the quarterly sessions was to facilitate the group in processing any issues or concerns they were having, and to assist them in continuing to build their mentoring skill sets. Following our December session, Karen asked if I had a few minutes to talk. "Sure, what's up?" I asked. "I guess I'm not sure what's going on, and that's part of the problem." "Okay, are there parts of the problem that you can define?" I asked. "Yes, the part that's bothering me the most is that I am not happy with where my relationship is at with Judy."

Karen went on to describe how Judy had been a student teacher in her building the previous school year, and how she had served as her cooperating teacher. She described the great job that Judy had done and how everyone was thrilled with her hiring. "I volunteered to serve on the search committee because I was so anxious about her getting the job. After she was offered the position and I was assigned to be her mentor, I couldn't have been more excited." Karen went on to describe how things had not turned out the way she had anticipated. "I don't know what is happening. All I know is that it feels like there is a distance between us that wasn't there before. I don't know, I was thinking this morning driving to school that maybe I am trying too hard." When I asked her to explain, she went on to describe how she was worried that perhaps she was still treating Judy like a student teacher. "I stop in her room every morning just to make sure that everything is okay, and to see if she has any problems or concerns. I know how busy she is, so I try to help her remember some of the important deadlines and meetings that can slip through the cracks." Before I had a chance to interject another probe, Karen said, "I'm thinking about backing off for a while. Maybe she thinks I'm trying to be a mother hen." "I doubt that, but it might be worth trying," was my reply.

In March, Karen arrived early for our quarterly meeting. "Thanks for helping me last time. Things have really improved." When I asked what happened, she described how she did "exactly what we talked about." She had backed off and made a concerted effort to wean herself from her daily visits with Judy. Karen described how, weeks later, she was in her classroom after school grading papers when Judy entered the room with tears in her eyes. She had just come from a meeting with a difficult colleague who she felt had embarrassed her in front of her grade-level teammates. Karen of course recognized that Judy was in need of some emotional support, and the pair sat and talked for almost an hour. By the end of the hour, they had developed a strategy for dealing with the problem and could, according to Karen, even begin to see some humor in the situation. "Things have been much better between us since then. It feels the way I hoped it would."

Processing the above story from a developmental mentoring perspective, there are actually two mentoring stories to be analyzed. First, there is the relationship between Karen and Judy, and second the interactions between Karen and me. It is perhaps clear now that Karen, despite her well-intentioned efforts, was in fact working in a counterproductive way by employing directive communications with a highly committed, responsible beginning teacher. By her own admission, she was trying too hard to make sure that Judy had all the information she needed to be successful in her job. The problem was that Judy already had the information and was functioning well. The daily reminders and repeated expressions of concern were eventually interpreted by Judy as signs of a lack of confidence in her ability. By Karen's own report, she was not directly telling Judy what to do, or how to do it. In fact, she was asking more questions than she was giving directives. What is important to note is that the repeated questions probably felt like mild directives from Judy's perspective. What is most significant is Karen's sensitivity to Judy's reactions. With time, she began to sense that something was not going well. Even more important, she looked first at herself in an effort to try to understand what was happening. In true high-performance mentor fashion, she reflected on her own communication behaviors and made a reflective decision to try a different approach. Imagine how easily she could have blamed Judy for the problem and lost her commitment to their relationship! In the end, when confronted with a personal crisis, Judy knew that Karen would provide the understanding she needed and was willing to openly share her dilemma and hurt.

Turning to my own behavior as described in the story, you may well have recognized that I chose a very nondirective approach with Karen. I did so for a number of reasons. First, my personal history of working with her told me that she was a highly committed and thoughtful mentor who was quite capable of self-direction. Second, as she began to share her problem, it immediately became clear that she had already given it considerable thought, and in fact had plotted a possible solution. I did little more than listen, ask a clarifying question or two, and finally encourage her to try her plan. It is interesting to note that, from Karen's perspective, I had helped her. In fact, I had. I helped her by employing communication behaviors that matched her developmental stage and that allowed her to be a self-directing problem solver.

To Guide or Not to Guide

Reflecting on my description of Allen and his efforts to guide my friend Scott and me, it's apparent that a number of things went awry. First, we quickly got the sense that he was more interested in impressing us with his knowledge and skill than he was in helping us develop our knowledge and skill. My honest sense was that he was not aware that we were interpreting his behavior in this way. I believe he had the *illusion* that he was connecting with us, when in fact he was not. Second, he seemed unable to read our nonverbal signals, even when they were sent loud and clear. To be honest, I felt a little guilty when conducting the "experiment" on him described earlier, but I was desperate. Finally, Allen's approach was perhaps most ineffective because it did not meet our developmental needs. We were highly committed students capable of thinking with him about many aspects of fly fishing. Perhaps we had seen too many TV shows that portrayed guides and their clients fishing together and enjoying the experience while they learned. I guess that is my way of saying we were looking for a more collaborative approach.

COMMUNICATION INDICATORS

The High-Performance Mentoring Framework includes five indicators related to effective communication. Collectively considered, they represent some of the keys that can open the doorways to meaningful dialogue between a mentor and a beginning teacher. Because this chapter has focused primarily on one of the five indicators, a few words about each seem warranted. The five indicators for *Reflects on Interpersonal Communications and Decisions* are:

1. Reflects on what, where, when, and how to communicate with the mentee

2. Adjusts communication style to the developmental needs of the mentee

3. Respects the confidentiality of the mentor-mentee relationship

4. Self-discloses regarding one's own professional challenges

5. Models effective helping relationship skills

Reflects on What, Where, When, and How

High-performance mentors are reflective communicators. They recognize that communication is the critical function of their work. Consequently, they think about such issues as whether they should initiate a conversation on a specific topic, or whether they should perhaps wait for the mentee to bring it up at a later date. When they do engage in dialogue with their beginning teachers, they often think later about how things went and whether there are any issues that need to be revisited. They periodically think about the context in which conversations take place, recognizing that physical surroundings can be an important factor in communication. Whereas some conversations might be appropriate in the teachers' lounge, others might be better suited for a more private setting. To summarize, I like to say that high-performance mentors do not act like interpersonal bulls in the china shop of first-year teachers. They are not reckless with their words, pushy with their ideas, or insensitive to the damage that they might cause.

Adjusts Communication Style

This particular communication attribute has been the focus of this chapter. The very best mentors understand that beginning teachers are developmentally different and consequently require different forms of communication. Just as in classroom teaching, what works one year may not work in another. I personally have found Glickman's theory (1985) to be a most appropriate framework for thinking about how I can be most helpful in dealing with different people in my personal as well as my professional life. It helps me recognize when I am sharing too many of my own ideas, when I need to present my view, or when it would be most helpful to actually direct someone's behavior. When things do not go well conversationally, I have a way of processing my communication behaviors and reflecting on whether they were appropriate.

Respects Confidentiality

Mentoring relationships are built on the bedrock of trust. In order to be truly helpful, mentors must create an environment in which beginning teachers are willing to share their problems and their needs. Most mentoring programs consequently view the mentor-mentee relationship as a confidential one, in which the mentor does not share information about the mentee with colleagues, and especially with administrators who might use the information in the evaluation process. This is not the case in all mentoring programs, so it is important that both mentors and mentees are clear about this issue. It has been my experience that for every administrator who seeks information on a beginning teacher, there is a mentor who volunteers it. A potentially fruitful relationship can be destroyed early on by a simple comment that was shared in confidence but makes its way back to haunt the beginning teacher. We will take a more detailed look at this issue in Chapter 6.

Self-Discloses Regarding One's Own Professional Challenges

Mentor teachers who are willing to share their professional problems and challenges endear themselves to beginning teachers, who become more comfortable in sharing their own struggles. One is far less likely to share a problem with someone who projects an image of having no issues of their own. If a beginning teacher, for example, is describing a problem she is having with an angry parent, the good mentor is likely to acknowledge her own ongoing efforts to handle such situations better. The key for the mentor is to keep the focus on the mentee's problem, and not turn the conversation into a discussion of the mentor's problem.

Models Effective Helping Relationship Skills

As alluded to at the beginning of this chapter, volumes have been written about this indicator. Several years ago, I decided to explore the literature on helping relationships and discovered several insights that I found particularly poignant. For me, they serve as powerful reminders of some of the most important aspects of being truly helpful. One of my favorites is from Rogers (1958), who wrote: "By a helping relationship, I mean a relationship in which at least one of the parties has the intent of promoting the growth, development, maturity, improved functioning, and improved coping with life of the other" (p. 8). For me, the key word is "intent," and intentionality must be communicated. When beginning teachers come to believe that you truly have the intention of helping them, many good conversations are sure to follow.

QUESTIONS FOR REFLECTION ON COMMUNICATING

- Are you content with the frequency of your conversations with your beginning teacher?
- Are your conversations occasionally focused on the substantive aspects of teaching and learning? Or, do they tend to be mostly about the superficial or more trivial aspects of teaching?
- How would you characterize the level of commitment of your beginning teacher? Is it low, moderate, or high?
- How would you characterize the level of abstraction of your beginning teacher? Is it low, moderate, or high?
- Given your responses to the preceding two questions, do you feel that your mentoring behaviors and communications are appropriately matched to the developmental level of the beginning teacher?
- When in a conversation with your beginning teacher, do you find yourself trying hard to "hear what isn't being said"?
- Do you endeavor to avoid the illusion of understanding by trying to ensure that you understand and are understood?
- Finally, can you honestly say that you have the intention of being a truly helpful force in the life of a beginning teacher? If so, do you feel that you have adequately communicated that intention by your words and actions?

6

Coaching

Manager is a title. It does not guarantee success.
Coaching is an action, not a title, and actions will result
in successes.

—Catherine Pulsifer

A good coach will make players see what they can be
rather than what they are.

—Ara Parseghian

My father gave me the greatest gift anyone could give
another person; he believed in me.

—Jim Valvano

Teachers, at their very best, are intellectuals. They live in the world of ideas, constantly challenged to find new and better ways to engage their students in a manner that will ignite their imaginations and fire their desire to learn. This intellectualizing is just as true for the kindergarten teacher as it is for the advanced placement physics teacher. The challenge is the same. And, it is a complex and monumental one that caring and committed teachers pursue throughout their teaching lifetimes. To make things even more daunting, teachers endeavor to live this life in complex school cultures, where social, political, and economic forces can combine to challenge the spirit and break the heart. High-performance mentors understand this reality and coach beginning teachers in a way that recognizes both their dreams and the challenges that can shatter them.

The preceding portrayal of the teacher's world has significant implications for the work of mentor teachers, and for their efforts to coach beginning teachers to experience professional success and personal satisfaction in that world. If teaching is a fundamentally intellectual enterprise, then high-performance mentors should employ coaching strategies that help beginning teachers focus on the cognitive aspects of their work, helping them refine and expand the ways in which they process the acts of planning, facilitating, and assessing teaching and learning experiences. If teaching is not only cognitively challenging, but emotionally demanding as well, then high-performance mentors should coach beginning teachers in a manner that respects the very personal dimension of being a teacher. To help meet these two important goals, we will explore three theoretical models that I have found helpful for informing and guiding the coaching process. Those models are cognitive coaching, coaching for confidence and competence, and coaching as cognitive apprenticeship. Before exploring those models and their practical applications, just a few words about the relationship of mentoring and coaching seem warranted.

RELATIONSHIP OF MENTORING TO COACHING

For many people, coaching is a word that can carry considerable baggage. Depending on one's own experience as a coach, or as one who has been coached, that history may be positive or negative. For example, I often encounter mentors-in-training who do not like to think of themselves as coaches because they view coaching as being an essentially directive process, wherein someone in a position of authority tells a performer what to do, or not to do. "It is not my job to tell a beginning teacher how to teach," they argue. Instead, they might add, "it is my job as a mentor to help them find their own way." Such perspectives often emerge from personal interpretations of the word "coach" and its relationship to the word "mentor."

In my mind, the very best mentors are good coaches, and the very best coaches are good mentors. I personally differentiate the two terms in the following way. To mentor another is to provide the help necessary for the novice to find *satisfaction* and *success* in the field to which he or she aspires. To coach someone, in contrast, is to help him or her acquire and refine the *knowledge and skills required for enhanced performance* in that field. To state it in a different way, I might argue that the work of the mentor is more concerned with the holistic needs of the beginning teacher—including his or her social and emotional needs and personal concerns—whereas coaches are more concerned with technical proficiency. Anyone who has mentored a beginning teacher, however, is likely to take issue with this distinction, arguing that mentors must focus on helping novice teachers acquire technical proficiency. Similarly, anyone who has ever coached an athlete, actor, or musician will argue convincingly that good coaches must also be excellent motivators who know how to read and meet the personal needs and concerns of individual performers.

If you find the preceding discussion of the relationship between mentoring and coaching tedious or unnecessary, it may be because you have already struggled with these issues at a personal level. If that is the case, you have done some important work that has likely influenced your personal performance as a mentor teacher. In contrast, if you found the discussion interesting or provocative, it may suggest that there is still work to be done to clarify your roles and responsibilities as a mentor teacher.

COGNITIVE COACHING

By the way, if it occurred to you that the very best classroom teachers mentor and coach their students every day, this may bring new and important insight to the term *mentor teacher*. This is one way to help resolve the dichotomy that I may have created by proposing alternative definitions of mentor and coach. In many ways, this same dichotomy is beautifully reconciled in the writings of Costa and Garmston (1994) and their work on cognitive coaching, in which they describe the coach as a mediating agent dedicated to helping valued people improve their "states of mind" so that they might enhance their capacity to modify themselves.

The cognitive coach uses a host of communication tools and strategies to promote self-reflection and self-directed growth; but the two most important ones, trust and rapport, should be in every mentor teacher's toolbox as well. I highly encourage mentor teachers interested in improving their mentoring skills to be trained in cognitive coaching. Information about workshops can be acquired at http://www.cognitivecoaching.com. The five states of mind that are the focus of cognitive coaching are worthy of further exploration by anyone dedicated to becoming a high-performance mentor. Table 6.1 introduces each state of mind by describing opposing ends of a continuum. Certainly, each of us can remember what it feels like to be in those lower states of mind, and hopefully in the higher ones as well.

I share the following story to help illustrate how the five states of mind can play out in practice, and how a caring and committed mentor can help convey a mentee toward higher states of mind. It is a story shared with me by a sixth-grade social studies teacher. Janine had been teaching for 18 years and had had the opportunity to mentor beginning teachers on three previous occasions. In each of those previous mentoring situations, the mentees were in their early twenties and had recently graduated from college. Janine's story, however, focused on her latest mentoring experience, in which she was assigned to mentor a 48-year-old beginning teacher who had just retired from the United States Navy. Jon was a highly decorated Navy SEAL and in his final years of service taught American military history at the United States Naval Academy. Previously, he trained new Navy SEALs in jungle survival

Table 6.1   The Five States of Mind in Cognitive Coaching

The Mentee's State of Mind	From	Toward
Efficacy	An external locus of control	An internal locus of control
Consciousness	Lack of awareness of self and others	Awareness of self and of others
Craftsmanship	Vagueness and imprecision	Specificity and elegance
Flexibility	Narrow, egocentric views	Broader and alternative perspectives
Interdependence Concern	Isolation and separateness	Connection to and for the community

SOURCE: Adapted from Costa and Garmston (1994).

and hand-to-hand combat techniques. As it turned out, Jon was an old friend and high school teammate of Janine's husband Tom.

In the initiation phase of their relationship, Janine called Jon in early August and invited Jon and his wife to dinner. The evening went well enough, but there was no talk of school as Jon and Tom swapped sports and military stories late into the evening. Although she felt good about seeing Jon and Tom reunited, Janine also felt that she had made no progress in initiating the mentoring relationship. As the evening wound down and the good-byes were shared, Janine told Jon to feel free to call her if he had any questions or needed any help getting ready for the start of school. Two weeks later, the school year started and since Janine had not heard from Jon, she decided to stop by his room and once again offer her support. "Let's just say it didn't go as I had planned," Janine began. "When I asked if there was anything I could do to help, he simply said, 'Nope, everything is under control.'" He thanked her again for dinner and then switched the conversation to Tom's plan to sell his business, a local hardware store. Janine went on to explain that after she got over her initial surprise, she began to think that there was no reason to be concerned. She was also honest enough to admit that she wasn't quite sure of what her next mentoring move would be. During the next 9 weeks she reported making several other attempts to see if Jon had any specific needs or questions. Each approach was turned away with polite disregard. "I have to admit I was initially frustrated by his behavior. After a while I began to feel self-conscious about the whole thing." Janine went on to explain that after a few days she began to realize that she was allowing her own feelings to get in the way of the mentoring process. She decided to take what she described as a "low-key and friendly" approach. She ate lunch at Jon's table whenever possible, but kept the conversation on topics of general rather than professional interest. Then, one December evening, Janine received a call from Jon asking if it would be okay to meet with her sometime during the holiday break.

When they met at a local coffee shop a week later, Janine could not have been more surprised. Jon began by explaining that he was thinking about not returning for the second half of the year. He went on to explain that teaching seventh graders had turned out to be a lot more difficult than he had anticipated. After overcoming her initial shock, Janine began the process of helping Jon process his feelings and develop a plan of action. As it turned out, that action plan included Jon's desire to take full advantage of Janine's experience and expertise. I am happy to report that Jon did return to school in January, and with Janine's help was able to address many of the problems and concerns that had him on the brink of resignation. Today, he is still on the job and enjoying his new career.

Processing Jon's story in light of the five states of mind, it is entirely possible that he began his new work with a rather narrow and perhaps egocentric view of teaching. In other words, he was not positioned cognitively, at the time, to think flexibly and entertain multiple perspectives on his new work.

With regard to interdependence, he felt increasingly isolated as he shut himself off from Janine's offers of assistance. As he told Janine that evening, "I think I let pride get in my way." As the first weeks of school unfolded, he had to face the reality that many of his methods were not working. As he confronted these issues of craftsmanship, he gradually felt less and less in control. By his own admission, he began the process of blaming his students and their parents for his ineffectiveness, moving to an external locus of control. Fortunately, he gradually became more aware of himself and the impact his behaviors were having on his wife and on his students. It was this awareness that eventually led him to make the call to Janine. It was a call he waited 4 months to make, but it was the call that made all the difference in the world.

COACHING FOR CONFIDENCE AND COMPETENCE

I have a 45-minute drive from my home to the university each day and consequently have become a fan of audio books and training programs. A few years ago, I was listening to a series of tapes by Kenneth Blanchard (1993) and discovered an interesting way of thinking about the coaching of beginning teachers. He was speaking about stages of skill development, and how learners need to be aware of what stage of skill development they are in, and what kinds of help they need. Hersey and Blanchard (1974) were the developers of situational leadership theory.

In this particular program, Blanchard was describing a new take on situational leadership, which he described as situational self-leadership. The central idea was that employees need to take responsibility for their own learning and seek out the specific kinds of help they need, based on an honest self-assessment of their level of skill development. What appealed to me was the idea that mentor teachers could introduce this theory to beginning teachers and then invite them to use the model as a way of thinking about their relationship and the coaching process. In such a scenario, mentors and mentees would both assume responsibility for the coaching relationship and share a common framework for thinking about their work.

The basic theory that anchors situational self-leadership is that there are four levels of skill development that are a function of the "confidence" and "competence" that a person possesses with regard to a specific task. The corollary of this claim is that each of the four levels requires different types of coaching strategies. The four general types of need are technical advice; feedback and emotional support; encouragement; and autonomy and peer dialogue. See Figure 6.1.

When examining the model, it is important to remember that the four levels of skill development are not generalized categories based on some holistic assessment of the beginning teacher's performance. Instead, they are levels of skill development that can vary depending on the specific skill or task in question. For example, the same beginning teacher might be an enthusiastic beginner with regard to differentiating

Figure 6.1   Four Levels of Skill Development of Beginning Teachers

	Level 3 *Reluctant Performer* Needs: Encouragement	Level 4 *Independent Achiever* Needs: Autonomy and Peer Dialogue
	Level 2 *Disillusioned Learner* Needs: Feedback and Emotional Support	Level 1 *Enthusiastic Beginner* Needs: Technical Advice

Level of Mentee's Competence — LOW to HIGH (vertical axis)

LOW   *Level of Mentee's Confidence*   HIGH

SOURCE: Adapted from Blanchard (1993).

instruction, and a disillusioned learner with regard to student discipline. Concurrently, he or she might be a reluctant performer when it comes to integrating technology, and an independent achiever when it comes to employing cooperative learning strategies. With this understanding in mind, let's examine each of the levels of skill development and the kinds of coaching help that would be most appropriate for each level. As you think about each level, you might find it helpful to reflect on your personal history of skill development with regard to some specific skill you were trying to develop in either your personal or professional life.

Beginning Teachers as Enthusiastic Beginners

At Level 1, beginning teachers are trying to develop skill in a particular aspect of professional practice in which they have "high confidence," but they have "low competence" with regard to the specific skill. I recently had a conversation with a beginning teacher named Shelly who, after studying the model, told the story of her desire to develop a classroom Web site. "I love the idea of having my own Web site. I have a lot of exciting ideas about what I want it to look like and how I want to use it, but I don't know where to begin." She went on to describe that she was "pretty good at technology" but was "clueless" on how to build a Web site. Shelly's high confidence that she could learn about Web design, coupled with her low competence, makes her a perfect candidate for a directive coach who can teach her the technical skills she needs. Because her motivation is already high, the coach can concentrate on technical development and be less concerned about emotional support at this particular time.

When I asked Shelly if her mentor had been able to help her, she quickly responded that she had. "Yes, my mentor calls herself a 'technophobe' but she supported me by hooking me up with another teacher in the building who is helping me learn what I need to know." In this case, the mentor was not personally able to meet Shelly's needs as an enthusiastic beginner, but behaved in a high-performance way nonetheless. Helping beginning teachers reflect on when they are in the enthusiastic beginner stage of skill development can help both them and their mentors become more proactive about obtaining the technical coaching they need. To be a good teacher is to revisit this stage of skill development many times in a career. Mentors who openly share their own enthusiastic beginner experiences go a long way toward helping novice teachers adopt this important perspective. Beginning teachers who accept that it is perfectly normal to need technical advice and direct instruction open themselves to accelerated growth on the steep learning curve called "learning to teach."

Beginning Teachers as Disillusioned Learners

Because so many professional skills are difficult to implement in practice, it is easy to understand how an enthusiastic beginner can become a disillusioned learner. At Level 2, beginning teachers begin to lose their confidence as they confront the reality that they lack the high level of competence they are trying to achieve. This is a difficult place to be from a psychological perspective, especially if the person is at this level in several areas of professional practice. In fact, it is at this point that many beginning teachers begin to doubt themselves and their professional preparation, and in worst-case scenarios, begin to think about quitting.

For far too many years, this is how I felt with regard to playing golf, especially about hitting a driver. In fact, I gave the game up for more than 20 years. A couple of years ago, however, I found myself back in the enthusiastic beginner stage. With my confidence high, I bought new clubs and signed up for lessons. My coach was good at explaining the art of hitting a golf ball, and with his instructions I straightened out my drive. Unfortunately, a year later I was back to my old ways, and quickly lost confidence as I once again experienced incompetence from the tee. I needed what many beginning teachers need from their mentors when they become disillusioned learners. I needed a coach who could provide technical feedback in combination with a good dose of emotional support.

"I felt out of control, and to be honest, a little bit ripped off, if you want to know the truth," a beginning teacher named Steve explained in reaction to my explanation of being at the disillusioned learner stage of skill development. Steve was having a very difficult time managing student behavior in his high school science classroom. "You would think that after 4 years of college and student teaching I would have some better strategies for dealing with the craziness that I have to deal with every day." When I asked him if he was getting help from his mentor, Steve said, "No, he really has no idea how bad things are." He went on to explain that he had been reluctant to ask for help with something that he felt he should already know how to do. "Plus," he added, "I really don't want him to see how frustrated and angry I am about the whole thing."

What Steve needed was an empathic coach willing to serve as a facilitative listener who could acknowledge the complexity and challenge of the task while helping him develop the skills he needed. Unfortunately, his unwillingness to openly share his disillusionment cut him off from the technical feedback and emotional support that would have constituted the appropriate coaching response. High-performance mentors are highly aware that the inner life of the teacher is a critical aspect of professional performance. Consequently, they are careful observers of their beginning teachers, looking for unarticulated signs of tiredness, deflation, and disillusionment. When they judge it necessary, they employ conversational prompts that invite mentees to share such feelings. Finally, they periodically reveal their inner lives by sharing their own disappointments, as well as the coping strategies they use to deal with such feelings.

Beginning Teachers as Reluctant Performers

Can you think of some aspect of your personal or professional life where you possess the competence to perform a particular task, but for some reason have lost your confidence? If we are honest with ourselves, most of us can. When our competence is high and our confidence is low, we find ourselves at the reluctant performer stage. It is not uncommon for beginning teachers to experience this stage of skill development.

Christy was the first beginning teacher in an entry-year support session to identify with being a reluctant performer. She described how her mentor teacher had recently been encouraging her to use more problem-based learning activities with her eighth-grade social studies classes. "I had a great student teaching experience with a veteran teacher who was an expert at structuring problem-based learning [PBL] environments. By the time I left student teaching, I felt I had the knowledge and skill to use the techniques on my own." Christy went on to describe how she had become reluctant to use them in her first year of teaching. "I began to think that my success in student teaching was due to the structure the cooperating teacher had established. I don't know, I guess I just began to question whether my students could handle that kind of learning environment."

Earlier in the year, Christy had talked with her mentor about her student teaching experience and shared her enthusiasm for PBL. Remembering the spark that Christy had as she described her experiences, her mentor apparently decided to revisit the topic occasionally by asking Christy if she was doing any PBL yet. Over time, she became a cheerleader dedicated to encouraging Christy to get past her fears and do something that she was in fact competent to do. Christy finished her story by describing how she finally decided in March to design and implement a PBL unit. "The kids loved it and did a great job. Now they are always asking me when we are going to do another PBL."

All of us occasionally need a cheerleader, someone who encourages us to move past limited and inaccurate conceptions of our own abilities. High-performance mentors understand that beginning teachers are likely to have areas of professional practice in which they are capable but reluctant.

Through observation and conversation, they try to identify those areas and then provide the necessary encouragement.

Beginning Teachers as Independent Achievers

At the highest level of skill development, teachers not only have high confidence in their ability to perform a specific task, but they also have the competence to match. At first, one might be tempted to think that very few beginning teachers might be operating at the independent achiever level of skill development. In reality, it is not that uncommon for them to be at this level in one or more areas of professional practice.

Kevin was the first-year teacher with the memorable story about being an independent achiever. "I think that was probably me when it came to being organized. Organization is something I have always been good at." Kevin elaborated by describing how his mentor had been impressed with his "system," which integrated a personal digital assistant and his laptop computer. "I ended up teaching him how it worked. He just got a Palm Pilot last week and I am teaching him how to use it."

When beginning teachers are seen to be operating at the independent achiever level in a particular area, thoughtful mentors recognize that they do not need technical advice, emotional support, or encouragement. They understand that providing room for autonomous action may be the best approach. This is not to imply that they do not acknowledge or praise mentees for their success. They are wise enough to realize that affirming such confidence and competence can do no harm, and is likely to be appreciated, if not needed. One way in which such affirmation is powerfully communicated is by expressing an interest in learning more about how the novice does what he or she does so well.

One of the dangers for mentors with regard to independent achievement is to falsely conclude that high confidence and competence in one area of professional practice translate automatically to other areas. I am always a little concerned when I hear mentor teachers explain that their mentees are so good that they really do not need their help. It is hard for me to imagine that this is actually the case. As was pointed out earlier, skill development is highly situational. Given the complexity of teaching and the reality that most skills are learned in practice, it is highly unlikely that beginning teachers are not in need of coaching in many areas of professional skill.

COACHING AS COGNITIVE APPRENTICESHIP

A more conceptually complex model that can inform the coaching of beginning teachers is based on the theory of cognitive apprenticeship. This theory espouses that people learn how to "practice" by being engaged in learning environments where they have the opportunity to interact with veteran practitioners in the context of dealing with problems and issues representative of the real world of practice. Cognitive apprenticeship, while it maintains some of the qualities of traditional apprenticeships, differs with its heavy emphasis on revealing the covert, cognitive aspects of practice and treating those thought processes as the content to be studied and eventually acquired.

Six Cognitive Apprenticeship Strategies

Collins, Brown, and Newman (1990) identified six cognitive apprenticeship strategies, each of which has significant implications for mentor teachers desiring to improve or diversify their coaching methods. The six models, which we will explore in detail, are as follows:

1. Modeling

2. Coaching

3. Scaffolding

4. Articulating

5. Reflecting

6. Exploring

After describing each of the strategies in terms of how it might be employed in the context of a mentoring relationship, I will identify the challenges that mentors may confront in their efforts to do so.

Modeling

In cognitive apprenticeship theory, modeling does not mean what it may first appear to mean. Many mentors-in-training think immediately of inviting beginning teachers to their classroom, where their mentees can watch them as they "model" one or more teaching practices of interest. This can be a very helpful strategy, but does not qualify as "modeling" if the exercise ends with the mentor's performance and the mentee's observation of that performance. In order to be considered modeling in the cognitive apprenticeship sense of the word, the teacher would need to reveal her thought processes with regard to the practice or skill being examined. This process is essentially one of making private teaching thoughts public, or putting one's mind on display. The goal of this process is to help novices learn how to think about their work by revealing the complex and subtle nature of how teachers think as they engage specific problems or situations. In this way, the observed performance is important essentially because it becomes the gateway for a later exploration of specific behaviors of interest, and of the thought processes that influenced or triggered them.

One way to help beginning teachers move beyond the gateway of the observation is to invite them to make notes on those aspects of the performance that they would like to talk about from this perspective. In this case, the tables are turned, if you will, and it is the beginning teacher who asks the "what were you thinking when" questions. When mentors respond honestly and thoughtfully to such questions, they provide their mentees with important insights into the hidden world of teaching that every teacher knows but rarely articulates. As the conversation develops, attention may well turn to the beginning teacher's story of how he or she tends to think in similar situations or circumstances. In such dialogue, it is not necessary to deal with issues of right and wrong, or best and better.

Mentors desiring to experiment with modeling do not need to begin the process with the mentee observing them in the classroom. The strategy can be employed anytime the mentor believes that a beginning teacher might profit from such an approach. For example, a beginning teacher named Angie related how her mentor used the modeling strategy to help her decide how to handle a very difficult issue in parental relations. Angie had an angry phone conversation with the mother of one of her students, who accused her of destroying her daughter's self-esteem and love of school. The mother ended the call by telling Angie that she intended to call both the principal and the superintendent. As Angie described it, she was "paralyzed by the accusations and their threatening tone." She then described how she approached her mentor for support. "At first she just listened, and I could tell she knew what I was feeling." The mentor had of course taken such calls before and acknowledged the feelings they had triggered in her own mind. "What was really interesting was how we talked about how to make good decisions when you are emotionally upset." By the end of their meeting, Angie had some new concepts to plug into her thought processes. Detachment, taking a third-party perspective, and keeping the principal informed were three things that had not been part of her thinking. "What was great," Angie concluded, "is that she didn't tell me to do those things. She just described how she thinks when such things happen."

There are a couple of traps associated with modeling that clearly should be avoided. The first one occurs when mentors are overanxious or too aggressive with the strategy, which can leave mentees feeling like there is more focus on the mentor's thinking than on their own. This trap becomes even more dangerous when mentors employ it without first providing the social and emotional support that may be necessary to clear the mind for reflection. Imagine, if you will, Angie approaching her mentor and saying, "I can't believe what she just said to me. I have never been so humiliated in my life. I didn't know what to say. I mean, I knew what I wanted to say but I couldn't say it so I just hung up." In such a situation, empathy and understanding trump modeling as the first course of response. Once emotions have calmed, the mentor might employ the modeling strategy, acknowledging that she too has had many of the feelings the mentee expressed. The next step would be to move on to a deeper discussion of how she processes and manages such situations when they occur. From Angie's report, this is in fact how her mentor responded.

Coaching

Interestingly, coaching is a specific strategy in cognitive apprenticeship, and the one with which most mentors are familiar. The approach is different than modeling because it places the thinking of the beginning teacher at center stage. The role of the mentor is to use the observation as the opportunity to identify specific aspects of the performance, which later become the topics of conversation between mentor and mentee. In this approach, mentors invite beginning teachers to make their private teaching thoughts public in the same way that the mentor has already "modeled" with regard to her own practice. Coaching is a complex strategy and there are many pitfalls to be avoided. Each pitfall, however, serves as an important reminder of specific mentor practices and behaviors that can be employed to avoid that trap. Here are the key pitfalls that I have discovered over the years, followed by a brief explanation of each and how it might be avoided.

1. The workroom coaching trap

2. The evaluation trap

3. The interpretation trap

4. The time trap

5. The confidentiality trap

As you will quickly see, these five traps are closely related to one another. In fact, this is so much the case that triggering one is likely to spring another.

The Workroom Coaching Trap. The workroom coaching trap is one that actually prevents mentors from using the coaching strategy in their mentoring practice. It captures mentors who have little or no interest or experience in observing their beginning teachers in the act of teaching. As I have written previously (Rowley, 2005), such mentors tend to approach their work in the way that would be equivalent to the athletic coach who prefers not to watch his or her athletes perform in game situations. Coaching is limited to "locker room" coaching, where players self-report on their performances and coaches use those reports to drive the coaching process. This trap is most likely to be found in mentoring programs that place little value on observation as a mentoring function. In such cases, classroom observations are not encouraged or required. The trap is also frequently found in mentoring programs where observation is encouraged but mentors are not provided the relevant training they may need to build their coaching competence and confidence. When this is the case, the remaining traps loom large.

The Evaluation Trap. The evaluation trap is an easy trap to fall into if mentors are not careful. The problem essentially stems from the fact that most teachers, especially beginning teachers, tend to think that three words in the English language mean the same thing. The three words are supervision, evaluation, and observation. Whereas these words are obviously related, they are not synonymous. Mentors who fail to help their beginning teachers understand the subtle and not so subtle differences between these words are likely to experience problems in employing the coaching strategy.

I will never forget a story related by a mentor teacher from Michigan who, like his mentee, was a high school science teacher. The mentor was perplexed because every time he stepped foot into his mentee's classroom, the mentee would stop teaching. Unfortunately, this happened frequently because the only way into the science prep room was through the beginning teacher's classroom. "I don't know what to do," he began, "but it is uncanny. As soon as I open the door, it is just like someone flips a switch. He just stops, practically in mid-sentence." When I asked if his district required or encouraged mentors to observe beginning teachers in the classroom, he explained that it did not. When I probed as to whether he and the mentee had ever talked about the nature of their relationship with regard to evaluation, he said, "No, I just figured that somebody told him I wasn't his evaluator."

The simple reality is that most people, when being observed, believe they are being judged or evaluated. This tends to be particularly true for beginning teachers, many of whom have significant survival concerns about being accepted and respected for their performance. The point here is that mentors must be explicit in describing the purposes and goals of the observations that they would like to conduct. I cannot emphasize enough the desirability of doing this as early in the relationship as possible. Every mentor will develop his or her own way of addressing the issue. Personally, I like to say something like this: "The first thing I want you to know is that I am not your evaluator. It is not my job to rate or score you in any way. I do look forward, however, to being in your classroom and I hope that you will find the opportunity to be in mine as well. Or, if you like, we can both visit another teacher's classroom. My real hope is that we will have many chances to have good conversation about the work that both of us are trying to do every day. I think observation is one of the best ways to get the conversation going." As I wrote these words, they did not feel quite right, because they are more easily communicated in the presence of another. So, although the words may not appeal to you, I hope the message does. I encourage you to find your own words to deliver this important message, which will go a long way toward avoiding the evaluation trap.

The Interpretation Trap. The third trap mentors can fall into is the interpretation trap. Let us assume that you have successfully navigated around the first two traps, and find yourself in the classroom of your beginning teacher. Picture yourself, perhaps in the back of the room, watching the teacher and students. What are you doing? Whereas there are many possible answers to this question, they are not all consistent with the cognitive apprenticeship notion of coaching. In that approach, mentors would be looking for teacher and student behaviors and interactions that they believe would be the topics of good conversation. There is an important point to be made here. High-performance mentors would be using their veteran judgment to make decisions about what classroom phenomena might yield the greatest value and benefit if mined in the process of collegial dialogue, where beginning teachers are invited and encouraged to think out loud about their thoughts. The conversational lubricant that facilitates this process is the purely descriptive data that bring attention to the phenomenon of interest. What freezes or stops the process most often is the beginning teacher's sense that the observer has leaped to an "interpretation" of what occurred, without hearing their perspective. This occurs when mentors interpret classroom events through their own perceptual lenses. It is exacerbated when mentors are unaware that these lenses are in place.

There are a number of ways to avoid the interpretation trap. The first is to periodically remind yourself that it is the beginning teacher's thinking that is the focus of the process. Second, employ data collection processes that render descriptive data. There are many methods for observing classrooms that yield this kind of data. *Looking in Classrooms* (Good &

Brophy, 2000) contains an array of observation tools that are anchored to the research literature on effective teaching.

One of the most commonly employed methods for recording observations is the scripting method, in which the observer writes a narrative of classroom events. Using purely descriptive language, the observer captures the teaching and learning episode so that it can be re-created in the mind of the beginning teacher. When this is done properly, no praise or criticism is communicated, and no suggestions are offered in the written script. It is a thoughtful rendering, if you will, of what occurred and an invitation for beginning teachers to put their minds on display in the follow-up conversation. I will discuss scripting in greater detail later in this chapter, when we explore the role of observation in the coaching process.

The Time Trap. The coaching process is best carried out in the context of what has historically been referred to as the clinical cycle, wherein the observed teaching episode is preceded by a planning or pre-observation conference and followed by a post-observation conference. Meeting with beginning teachers in a pre-observation conference provides an excellent opportunity to employ other cognitive apprenticeship strategies, such as scaffolding, articulating, and exploring. Unfortunately, mentors sometimes feel as if they do not have the time to meet for the pre-observation conference. This is unfortunate, because failing to find the time for such a meeting increases the chance of the interpretation trap coming into play. Listening to a novice teacher talk about a lesson and describe the thought processes he or she employed to develop it can provide a rich opportunity for those mentors willing to spend the small amount of time it takes. A great deal can be accomplished in 15 minutes, especially if the mentor has the opportunity to study the teacher's lesson plan before the conference. From my perspective, such a conference honors planning as central to the work of good teaching, in addition to being the fair thing to do. Teachers have reasons for their actions and those reasons are better explained by the performer than interpreted by the observer.

The Confidentiality Trap. Most entry-year programs are based on mentors and beginning teachers working together in a confidential helping relationship where it is understood that mentors will not share information on their mentees with those responsible for evaluating those teachers. Nothing can kill the coaching process faster than the beginning teacher's belief that this confidence has been broken.

In a *confidential mentoring model,* mentors must understand that any assessment data they collect are formative in nature and are to be shared only with the beginning teacher in the context of the mentor relationship. In contrast, in a *peer assistance and review program model,* mentors and beginning teachers should both understand that performance assessment data collected in the coaching process can be both formative and summative and consequently may—or, in some programs, will be—used to inform decisions about retention or nonrenewal. Whatever the model, it is essential that all parties involved, especially the beginning teacher, are fully informed as to how, with whom, and for what purposes information will be shared.

Scaffolding

You may be familiar with the concept of scaffolding as a method that classroom teachers use to support students in learning to perform a task they are unable to complete on their own. Teachers, for example, sometimes use other students to provide the necessary support. Or, they may provide the scaffold themselves in any number of ways, including monitoring and feedback, the use of guided questions, conversational hints, and the list goes on. In a mentoring relationship, scaffolding can be employed in a variety of situations and settings, ranging from formal to informal conversations. However, it is most powerful when employed in the context of shared experience.

Some of the most powerful coaching opportunities occur in the context of a *shared experience* in which both mentor and beginning teacher engage in collaborative planning and teaching.

I personally believe that mentors should be strongly encouraged to engage in some kind of collaborative teaching experience with their mentees. Scaffolding in a co-teaching context occurs naturally and can go a long way toward building a positive mentoring relationship based on open communication and mutual respect. This is particularly true if mentors allow their beginning teachers to be full and contributing partners in the planning and instructional processes.

Unfortunately, far too many beginning teachers are not provided such opportunities because mentors are not encouraged or supported to employ this approach. Even when they are encouraged, many mentors typically resist the idea, pointing out that the beginning teacher does not teach the same subject matter or grade level—or, more frequently, that they do not have the time for such an initiative. Regarding time, it is hard for this writer to imagine a better use of a mentor's time. Regarding the grade level or subject matter excuse, a creative disposition is required. Why, for example, can't a sixth-grade mentor engage his students in studying a topic or conducting a project with a beginning teacher's fourth-grade class? For that matter, why can't a beginning high school social studies teacher and her English department mentor develop an integrated unit on some topic of common interest or importance?

Articulating

Mentors who employ this cognitive apprenticeship strategy value teacher thinking as being central to their work. Perhaps intuitively, they understand that the internal thought processes that drive teacher behavior are the real subject of interest. Consequently, they help their beginning teachers feel comfortable with the process of making tacit knowledge explicit so that it can be discussed and analyzed. They are good at drawing out the thoughts of their beginning teachers without making them feel as if they are being interrogated or evaluated. One technique they employ to prevent such feelings is being overt about their intentions at the beginning of the relationship. Expressing curiosity and interest in the hidden world of teacher thought is one way to set the stage. When such an expression of intent is followed by modeling on the mentor's part, beginning teachers often sense that they are being treated as true professionals responsible for making decisions in a complex, multidimensional environment. In such a conversational climate, the work of the teacher is honored as mentors provide the scaffolding to help novices move beyond simplistic and dualistic conceptions of professional practice.

One of the best opportunities for using the articulation strategy is when beginning and mentor teachers are involved in the problem-solving process, and mentors can invite mentees to articulate the ways in which they are conceptualizing, framing, processing, and responding to problematic situations or events. In such conversations, mentors have a great opportunity to gain insight into the beginning teacher's level of abstract thinking, which was discussed in Chapter 5. Such insights can occur only when mentors open a window into the inner world of teacher thought. Once such insights are acquired, mentors can adjust their communication behaviors to help scaffold the novice to higher and more abstract levels of professional thought.

Some of the pitfalls associated with the articulating strategy are problematic with other strategies as well. For example, asking too many questions aimed at prompting articulation can leave beginning teachers feeling as if they are under attack. In addition, the way in which questions are asked can also be an issue. For example, many mentors-in-training, when asked to practice this strategy, use "why questions," believing that they offer a good way to invite deep thinking. Although such questions are important because they invite an exploration of motive and purpose, they are often perceived as evaluative in nature. When confronted with "why questions," some people immediately feel a need to defend their actions. Most of us can relate to this phenomenon in our communications with spouses, children, relatives, and friends. If we are honest, we can probably relate to both asking and being asked "why."

Reflecting

One way to think of the cognitive apprenticeship strategy of reflecting is to conceptualize it as the process of "abstracted replay." In this approach, mentors invite and encourage beginning teachers to think out loud as they revisit a specific event in professional practice, including classroom teaching episodes.

Many mentors tend to think of this strategy as being most appropriate in the post-observation conference as a vehicle for promoting reflection after a teaching episode. In fact, the strategy is equally well applied in the context of a pre-observation conference as a strategy for exploring the thought processes that were at work as the teacher planned the lesson.

Mentors can prompt reflection in a variety of ways by employing a number of different methods. One of the most effective ways to promote reflection is to invite beginning teachers to engage in the process of reflection as stimulated by some "artifact" of interest. Such artifacts might be volunteered by the mentee or created with the support of the mentor. Whatever the case, the advantage of the artifact-driven approach is that it provides a specific and authentic representation of the teacher's practice. For example, a sample of student work, a lesson plan, a teacher-created assessment, an audio- or videotaped record of a teaching episode, or a mentor's script from a classroom observation all have great potential to stimulate reflection and collegial dialogue.

The purpose of using any of the artifacts described above is to help the novice revisit the thought processes that were at work when the artifact was captured. Mentors block this process if they do not allow the beginning teacher the first opportunity to think out loud. This happens even when mentors are well intentioned and feel the need to affirm the beginners by telling them that they did a good job before hearing the mentees' perspective. A word of caution is necessary here, as I don't mean to imply that the mentor should begin with the question: "So, how do you think it went?" Such a question, although very popular with those who evaluate teachers, is not a particularly good place to begin promoting reflection. The problem is that it invites the beginner to make a holistic evaluation of a teaching episode, in which it is most likely that some things went well, others not so well, and perhaps something even went poorly. It also shares with the "why question" the effect of inviting a defensive posture. Many teachers, when asked "How do you think it went?" are immediately at work trying to guess how the questioner thought it went. This inclination leads to tangled, strategic thinking that is often more political than clinical in nature. My preferred way to begin is to simply ask the beginning teacher what he or she would prefer to talk about first. Where would you like to start? What is interesting to you?

One of the most interesting aspects of taking this approach is discovering how frequently the beginning teacher will choose to talk about the thing that was of the greatest interest to you. In contrast, if the mentee is unwilling or unable to respond to such a prompt, you are still gaining important insight. For example, when this happens to me, I often wonder if perhaps I have done something to create defensiveness or mistrust. Or, I might begin to develop a hypothesis regarding the beginner's reflective capacity or level of abstract thinking. Such hypotheses can then be tested with new prompts or communication behaviors. If these fail, I might initiate the conversation by pointing out some specific aspect that intrigued or interested me.

When thoughtfully employed, audio and video artifacts can be among the most powerful tools for promoting teacher reflection. The potential pitfall occurs when mentors fail to consider the sensitivity that many people have with regard to listening to or watching themselves. For every beginning teacher who thinks taping her class is a great idea, there is one who gets physically ill thinking about the prospect. It has been my experience that mentors do not need to watch a videotape *with* their beginning teacher. Much reflection can be stimulated when the novice takes the opportunity to watch the tape alone. In almost every case, mentors will discover that their mentees will volunteer their thoughts the following day.

Thoughtful mentors anticipate these initial comments and use them to deepen the process of reflection. By the way, I am a big fan of audiotaping, because it is a more covert method for capturing classroom interactions. A tape recorder sitting on a teacher's desk can be activated at any time without students being aware and possibly altering their behaviors. Listening to such a tape on the way home from school is a great way to stimulate the reflective process. The role of the mentor is to suggest the strategy and then offer the invitation to talk after he or she has listened to the tape alone.

Exploring

In some respects, one could view exploring as the strategy that every mentor hopes he or she will eventually be able to employ. In this approach, mentors encourage beginning teachers to assume responsibility for independent problem solving and to follow their own interests and professional curiosities. This is not to imply that mentors abandon their role or lessen their commitment when encouraging their mentees to become self-directed explorers. To the contrary, they do so in a manner that communicates to the novice teacher their continued interest in their professional development. Thus, the approach becomes a powerful way of validating and affirming the new teacher's developing confidence and competence.

The challenge for mentors is in knowing when to employ the strategy. In some respects, this cuts to the question I so often hear from mentors, namely: "When do I push, and when do I pull back?" Of course, classroom teachers struggle with this question on a daily basis as they thoughtfully consider the readiness of students. In similar fashion, thoughtful mentors do the same.

THE ROLE OF OBSERVATION IN COACHING

Observation is a coaching process that is at the very heart of a mentor's efforts to help a beginning teacher acquire and develop the technical skills and cognitive processes related to successful teaching and enhanced student learning. The goal of any observation, regardless of what form it might take, is to stimulate meaningful conversation between mentors and mentees about the work that they both do on a daily basis. In others words, whether the mentor observes the mentee or the mentee observes the mentor—or perhaps the mentor and mentee together watch another teacher—the goal remains the same: deep dialogue about the beliefs and behaviors that constitute one's professional practice. I have an abiding faith that when mentors and mentees engage in this kind of dialogue they both benefit in significant ways, and the students are the ultimate beneficiaries. Anyone who has ever mentored a beginning teacher, however, is likely to understand that this is not always an easy goal to achieve.

Many forces and factors conspire to interfere with the process at any number of points. For example, some mentees are reluctant to be observed for fear they will be judged or evaluated by their mentor. In contrast, some mentors do not believe that observation is an important mentoring function, or feel ill-prepared to conduct a classroom observation. To complicate matters further, mentors and mentees may work in the context of an entry-year program that holds no expectations regarding classroom observations. And, of course, time is frequently cited as a barrier. Mentors and mentees who do manage to engage in some type of observation experience may encounter still other roadblocks. Mentors, for example, are sometimes frustrated by their mentee's seeming unwillingness or inability to engage in open and reflective dialogue. In contrast, mentees are sometimes reluctant to share their thoughts because they believe they will not be accepted or respected by their mentors. In my view, all these roadblocks, as well as many others, can be navigated by caring and committed mentors who accept their mentees as developing persons who are living and learning at different levels of ersonal and professional development. The frameworks for thinking about the development of beginning teachers that were shared in Chapter 4 can go a long way to help mentors adopt this important perspective. Similarly, the developmental approach to mentoring, advanced in Chapter 5, can help mentors become more thoughtful about the nature of their communications. Finally, reflecting on beginning teachers as having different needs based on their levels of confidence and competence, as described earlier in this chapter, can also help mentors clear the roadblocks to good conversation.

Clinical Observation

As stated above, observations can take many forms. On the following pages, however, I focus on one particular approach—that of the mentor observing the mentee in the context of the clinical cycle, which includes a pre-observation conference, the classroom observation itself, and a post-observation conference. Clearly, this approach to observation is one of the most commonly employed and potentially one of the most powerful. Originally proposed by Goldhammer (1969) as a method for conducting teacher evaluations, the clinical cycle works equally well as a mentoring process, as long as the mentor and mentee have a shared understanding that it is not being used to conduct a summative evaluation of the beginning teacher's performance. This is especially important, because the process closely mirrors that which is used by many principals when conducting teacher evaluations. Consequently, it is important that mentors explain to mentees that whereas the methodology is similar, the end purpose is different. Failing to help beginning teachers understand that the purpose is to stimulate dialogue about teaching and learning can often spring the evaluation trap described earlier in this chapter. Before sharing some specific strategies for each phase of the clinical cycle, here are few general thoughts to keep in mind.

1. *The focus of the clinical cycle can be broad or narrow.* In other words, it can take a very holistic perspective on the teaching and learning episode to be observed, or it may focus on one or more specific aspects of the lesson. Early in a mentoring relationship, for example, mentors might be more

inclined to take a broad view of a teaching episode, whereas later in the relationship they might begin to focus more tightly on specific teaching and learning behaviors.

2. *The focus of the observation should be negotiated.* One of the hallmarks of the clinical cycle approach is that it involves the mentor and mentee in a shared study of the mentee's professional practice. Consequently, mentors and mentees should discuss what might be the appropriate focus for any given observation. Equally important, they should also discuss the observation method and tools that the mentor will use to make a record of the teaching episode.

3. *The mentor's role in the process, particularly the pre- and post-observation conferences, should be customized to meet the developmental needs of the mentee.* High-performance mentors understand the importance of adjusting their communications to meet the needs of their mentees, as discussed in Chapter 5. For example, when working with beginning teachers who have demonstrated high levels of abstract thinking, they tend to take a more nondirective approach to the conference.

The Pre-Observation Conference

The pre-observation conference provides mentors with the opportunity to gain important insights regarding the lesson to be observed. And, of course, it provides mentees with the opportunity to reflect on the various decisions that were made in the planning of the lesson. From my perspective, mentors should feel obliged to conduct the pre-observation conference before observing their mentees. This sense of obligation should spring from an understanding that it is the fair thing to do and that it ultimately can prevent them from misinterpreting or misjudging any number of things they might happen to observe. Just recently, I was training a group of mentors when one of the workshop participants reinforced this point by describing how he had learned this lesson the hard way. While observing his mentee without having conducted a pre-observation conference, he became concerned with the fact that the beginning teacher was holding a paper in front of his mouth while delivering the lesson. What made him especially concerned was that he knew one of the students had a severe hearing problem and received most of his information by lip reading. In the post-conference, the mentor quickly made the suggestion that the teacher needed to break the habit of holding papers in front of his face while talking. He was rather embarrassed when the mentee calmly explained that he was holding the paper in front of his mouth to hide a small microphone that he was using to communicate with the hearing-impaired student, who was wearing an experimental, in-the-ear receiver!

The good pre-observation conference focuses not only on the lesson to be observed, but on the thoughts and feelings of the beginning teacher as well. This can be accomplished by employing guiding questions designed to gain insight into both areas of interest. Here is a simple set of possible questions that can help mentors better understand the lesson itself. They are organized around five basic themes: students, goals, methodology, sequence, and evaluation.

1. Who are the learners I will be observing? What can you tell me about them? What is important for me to know about them?

2. What are the goals or objectives of this lesson? Where are you trying to take the students with this lesson?

3. What methods and materials will you be using? Are students familiar with these methods and materials?

4. Where does this lesson fit into your curriculum? What have students learned in the past that is related to today's lesson? How does today's lesson relate to what students will learn in the future?

5. When and how will you evaluate student learning as it relates to this lesson? How will you know that students learned what you hoped they would learn?

In contrast, here are some questions that can help mentors better understand their beginning teachers' states of mind with regard to the lesson.

1. How do you feel about this lesson?

2. Is there anything specific that you would like me to focus on during the observation?

3. Are there specific students you are concerned about with regard to this lesson?

4. Do you have any questions or concerns about the lesson that you would like to discuss?

When asking the above questions, mentors should do so in a way that communicates real interest in the lesson and genuine concern for the mentee.

Conducting the Observation

There are many methods for making a record of a teaching episode. Such methods include mapping or visual diagramming, coding, frequency counting, audio- or videotaping, and scripting. Because there is not space in this book to cover all these methodologies in-depth, I will concentrate on one of the most commonly used methods, that of scripting, or making a written record of the lesson. The primary goal in preparing a good script is to create a nonjudgmental record of the teaching episode that is free of the observer's interpretations. This is important for a couple of key reasons. First, presenting beginning teachers with such a document dramatically reduces the possibility that they will become defensive in the post-observation conference. Second, reviewing the judgment-free script encourages beginning teachers to replay the lesson in their minds, stimulating reflection and self-assessment. When mentors let their own assessments of the lesson bleed through on the script, the focus of discussion inevitably turns to the mentor's thoughts, as opposed to those of the mentee. It is important to note here that I am not devaluing the wisdom of mentors and the importance of their making suggestions or offering advice to their mentees. However, the script of the lesson is not the place to do this. For any readers old enough to remember the TV show *Dragnet*, the best advice for mentors who choose to script can be summarized in the words of Sergeant Joe Friday, who liked to say, "Just the facts ma'am, just the facts."

Here are a couple of ways that I like to think about the script. First, it is a gift that a mentor prepares for the mentee. This reminds us that the script is prepared for the beginning teacher as a way to help them think about their work, and not as a set of private notes that the mentor prepares for himself. Second, the script is essentially a conversational stimulant. The more factual it is, the more dialogue it is likely to promote. Finally, it is a game tape, not unlike those that are made of football games. The videotape of the quarterback's performance captures what transpired, free of judgment. The camera has no opinions. Here are 10 suggestions that should help mentors who are new to scripting as well as those who may have used the method in the past:

1. Accept the fact that you are not going to capture everything. Just as a video camera will miss some of the action, so will you.

2. Accept the fact that you will find it hard not to have judgments as you are scripting. This is not a problem as long as the statements that you write do not communicate those judgments.

3. Remember to focus on the students and their performances during the lesson, as well as on the performance of the teacher.

4. Experiment with capturing some of the verbal statements or interactions that occur, but don't feel obliged to write down everything the teacher says. A good script will often have some direct quotes as well as descriptions of what transpired.

5. Be particularly attentive to capturing important patterns of teacher or student behavior. These are often more significant than isolated occurrences.

6. Monitor your own behavior. It is very easy to become engaged or disengaged in what is occurring in the classroom and to stop scripting. If you catch yourself not writing for a period of time, pick it back up and don't worry about what you might have missed.

7. Remember that you are trying to create something that your beginning teacher can read. Therefore, slow down your writing so that you are sure it will be legible. Or, consider using a laptop computer to produce the script.

8. Use abbreviations to save you time and effort. For example, T can stand for teacher, MS for male student, and so on. Create whatever abbreviations you like, but be sure to explain them to your mentee when you give him or her the script.

9. Consider occasionally entering a time code in the margin of the script. For example, you might note the time the class began, the time when the teacher made the transition to small-group work, and the time when she began whole-group processing.

10. Experiment with the "wow, hmm, and oops" framework to help you decide what to script. I describe this method below.

Deciding What to Script

Two of the biggest frustrations mentors express when trying to create a script are related to suggestions 1 and 2. In other words, "I know I am missing stuff" and "It is hard not to have opinions" are the two most commonly heard complaints. In fact, I have heard them so often that I now offer the following advice, which many mentors have reported to be helpful. First, since you can never capture it all and feel that you are missing stuff, concentrate on capturing the *important stuff*. In my view, the important stuff can be viewed as falling into three categories, "wow, hmm, and oops," which really are a function of your professional judgments. For example, if you are scripting and suddenly find yourself impressed with something the beginning teacher—or one of the students— did or said, you had a "wow" moment and should be sure to capture the factual description of what occurred. This is important because it provides you the opportunity in the post-observation conference to praise or reinforce the observed behavior. Beginning teachers need specific praise and affirmation, so try not to miss opportunities to describe the wows! To be clear about what I am suggesting, the observed "wow" triggers a scripting entry, but the written entry itself is purely factual. In other words, the thought you have in your mind is positive, but the words that land on the page are purely descriptive. For example, let's say you observe a beginning teacher patiently rephrase a question to help a child successfully answer it in front of her peers. Your script entry might be: "T rephrases question twice. Roshanda answers correctly. T praises student." In the post-observation conference, you may then want to point to that incident and offer specific praise for the observed teacher behavior.

There are many things that occur in classrooms that observers find interesting, but do not fully understand. Such observations stimulate curiosity, for example, about what may have been going on in the mind of the beginning teacher, or what is the history of a particular student. Such "hmm" moments should stimulate mentors to capture descriptively the phenomenon that piqued their professional curiosity. Mentors who point to entries in the script that were the result of a "hmm" moment, and then ask their beginning teachers to help them understand the phenomenon of interest, go a long way to helping their mentees become reflective practitioners. And, mentors who appreciate the power of using the "hmm" moment are less likely to find themselves in situations like the one described by the mentor who immediately saw the papers held in front of his mentee's face as an "oh no."

Sometimes mentors observe something during a lesson that elicits their concern. In such moments, they find themselves saying "oops," or in some cases perhaps, "oh no." It is important for mentors to be very thoughtful about what is causing them to have such feelings. For example, are such feelings just the result of observing that the beginning teacher prefers a different approach or method than they do? Or, are they the result of a genuine concern that a teacher or student behavior is potentially self-defeating, counterproductive, or dangerous? In either case, writing a judgment-free description of the phenomenon of interest provides the opportunity to think more about it in preparation for the post-observation conference.

The Post-Observation Conference

Ideally, the post-observation conference should be held as soon as possible following the classroom observation, but not before the mentee has reviewed the script and reflected on what aspects of the lesson he or she would like to discuss. While the mentee is reading and reflecting on the script, the mentor should take the opportunity to do the same. How the mentor will approach the post-observation conference will be influenced by a number of factors, but primarily by her understanding of the beginning teacher's needs, dispositions, and developmental level.

Most teachers have had the experience of being in a post-observation conference with their principal where the first question asked is: "So, how do you feel the lesson went?" I suspect that this is a popular question because principals feel it provides teachers with an opportunity to offer their perspective on the lesson, and it does. On the other hand, starting with such a question can also set up a political dynamic because it invites the teacher to make a holistic assessment of the lesson. For example, the teacher may feel it would not be wise to say the lesson went well because she senses that the principal may feel otherwise. As an alternative, I advise starting a post-observation conference with the following two statements. First, simply ask the mentee: "Have you had a chance to look over the script? If he answers yes, then follow with: "Okay, where would you like to begin? Or, "All right, what would you like to talk about first?" Notice that such questions do not solicit a judgment, but rather are simple invitations to begin the dialogue. How a beginning teacher responds, or fails to respond, to such an invitation speaks volumes about his level of comfort with the mentor, his level of ability to reflect on his own practice, and his level of maturity, as well as his ability to think abstractly.

In some cases, beginning teachers will quickly take the opportunity to focus on one or more aspects of the lesson that are of particular interest or concern. In other cases, they will seem reluctant to do so, requiring the mentor to employ follow-up probes such as: "Was there anything about the lesson that surprised you?" Or, "Was there anything that you might do differently the next time you teach this lesson?" One of the wonderful things that often happens as a result of taking this approach is that beginning teachers will frequently want to talk about those phenomena that were of concern to the mentor. This is good news on two fronts, as it provides evidence of the mentee's ability to self-assess his or her own performance and saves the mentor from having to initiate dialogue about an "oops" or "oh no" concern.

One final piece of advice regarding the post-observation conference has to do with what I like to call the "mountain climbing questions." This approach requires mentors to answer three important questions regarding the post-observation conversation. The first question, "Is this really a mountain?" is designed to force mentors to think deeply about whether something they observed, and are perhaps concerned about, is in fact an important issue that needs to be discussed. I recently talked with a mentor who was very concerned that she had observed her mentee using candy to reward her fourth graders for good behavior. After we talked about what else she had observed, the candy-reward mountain seemed to fade away. The second question, "Which mountain should we climb first?" forces mentors to thoughtfully consider the needs of the mentee in terms of their relative importance. Making this decision can of course be done in concert with the mentee. Finally, mentors who ask themselves the question "Whose mountain is this anyway?" force themselves to reflect on whether they are trying to climb a mountain that has personal significance, but is of little interest to their mentee. Sometimes, of course, the mentee's lack of readiness to address a particular issue becomes secondary, and the mentor decides that the climb must begin. For example, a mentor who observes a pattern of teacher behavior that is patently unfair may choose to address the issue because she becomes convinced that the mentee is not aware of the behavior.

Videotaping and Audiotaping

When teaching mentors how to conduct classroom observations, I am often asked about the use of video- or audiotaping to make a record of the teaching episode. Frequently, the question takes the following form: "If we are trying so hard to be objective about what happened, why don't we just videotape the class?" In response, I first explain that I personally believe that videotaping or audiotaping a lesson are very effective methods for promoting reflection and dialogue with a beginning teacher. At the same time, I offer the following observations and suggestions. First, and perhaps most important, be mindful that many people have strong negative feelings about being taped. The reasons for this disposition vary from individual to individual. Some people, for example, do not like the sound of their voice, or the way they look on camera. Others report being nervous or anxious and being unable to perform in a normal way. In contrast, others seem to be largely unaffected and in fact like to hear or see themselves in action in the classroom. Given the reality of these differences, I offer the following suggestions:

1. Never plan to video- or audiotape beginning teachers without first discussing it with them and securing their permission.

2. Be aware that many schools and school districts have strict policies regarding the videotaping of students. Some, for example, require prior parental permission.

3. Understand that some teachers will not object to being taped as long as they know the tape will not be viewed by anyone but themselves. Therefore, do not assume that permission to tape is the same as permission for you to watch or listen.

4. Appreciate the fact that there is power in beginning teachers listening to or viewing a tape without you doing so. You can invite them to talk with you about their observations and still have meaningful dialogue.

5. If you are working with a beginning teacher who has a positive disposition toward being taped and processing the tape with you, take advantage of this openness to using these powerful tools, and offer to bring the sodas and popcorn.

Remember, whether you are writing a script, creating visual diagrams, mapping, or videotaping, the purpose is the same: creating a nonjudgmental record of the teaching and learning episode. How you use that record of evidence with your beginning teacher will vary widely from case to case. Returning to my analogy of the football game tape, imagine the coach who knows that his quarterback is a mature, reflective, and highly committed athlete with a high capacity for self-assessment and abstract thinking. Such a coach is likely to give such a player the opportunity to *break down* his own performance. In contrast, the coach who senses that a player cannot see the errors he is making, or has a limited capacity for self-analysis, may need to take a more collaborative or perhaps even directive role in the postgame conversation. Ultimately, the goal is to help convey new teachers to that place where they have an enhanced capacity for reflection and self-assessment, and a positive disposition toward continuous improvement.

COACHING INDICATORS

There five indicators for *Serves as an Instructional Coach* are:

1. Employs the clinical cycle of instructional support
2. Values the role of shared experience in the coaching process
3. Engages the mentee in team planning and team teaching whenever possible
4. Possesses knowledge of effective teaching practices
5. Models openness to new ideas and instructional practices

Employs the Clinical Cycle

High-performance mentors recognize that the clinical coaching cycle provides the process by which they can access the thinking of beginning teachers and see that thinking manifested in the classroom. They understand that the pre-observation and post-observation conferences are powerful opportunities for gaining insight into teacher cognition. They also recognize the clinical cycle as being a fair method for honoring teachers' thoughts, allowing them to observe the teaching and learning episode from an informed perspective.

Values the Role of Shared Experience

Coaching can happen anywhere and anytime mentors and beginning teachers share a personal or professional experience. Faculty or team meetings, professional conferences, the lunch table, and after-school events all provide mentors with opportunities to self-disclose their thoughts and feelings about issues of teaching and learning and invite their mentees to do the same. The conversations that flow from such shared experiences are often just as important as those that might occur in more formal coaching settings.

Engages in Team Planning and Teaching

High-performance mentors hold a conception of coaching that is not limited to the traditional observation-followed-by-feedback model. They look for opportunities to share planning and teaching experiences with their mentees in what might be called the player-coach model. They value this approach because it places them in authentic situations where they can think and act with their mentees as they work toward a common professional goal.

Possesses Knowledge of Effective Teaching Practices

High-performance mentors are knowledgeable about effective teaching practices and engage beginning teachers in discussions of those practices. In many entry-year programs, such discussions are driven by the research-based frameworks that are being used to drive state-mandated beginning teacher assessment programs. In addition, they are interested in the latest findings regarding what constitute best practices in various subjects and grade levels.

Openness to New Ideas

Mentors who are open to new ideas, especially those expressed by their beginning teachers, go a long way toward building a coaching relationship grounded in mutual trust. Communicating interest in beginning teachers' ideas can be one of the most powerful ways of affirming them as new members of the teaching community.

QUESTIONS FOR REFLECTION ON COACHING

- Do you agree that teaching is cognitively complex and emotionally demanding?
- Does your image of mentoring include the conception of coaching?
- If so, does that conception value the role of observation and shared experience in the coaching process?
- Do your coaching efforts attend to your mentee's needs with regard to both competence and confidence?
- Reflecting on the self-leadership model, at what level of skill development are you operating with regard to specific coaching behaviors?
- Have you sought out the types of help that would be most appropriate for the various skill levels you identified?
- Reflecting on the six cognitive apprenticeship strategies, can you identify one or more that you would like to experiment with in coaching beginning teachers?
- Are you a "workroom coach," or do you believe in the power of observation and shared experience in the coaching process?
- What strategies do you employ to avoid the "evaluation trap"?
- Do the beginning teachers with whom you work have a clear understanding of the role that confidentiality plays in the coaching process?

7

Learning

Only those who have learned a lot are in a position to admit how little they know.

—L. Carte

One of the reasons people stop learning is that they become less and less willing to risk failure.

—John Gardner

It is what we know already that often prevents us from learning.

—Claude Bernard

High-performance mentors are lifelong learners committed to the idea that those who teach must never cease to learn. Many with whom I have worked seem to have a natural sense of curiosity about their students and their lives, the instructional methods and resources they employ, and the content of what they teach. Perhaps equally important, they display significant motivation to learn more about beginning teachers and how to help them find success and satisfaction in their new careers. Many are highly reflective individuals who seem to be students of themselves, interested in their personal development with regard to being the best mentors they can be. Finally, they are visible learners who talk with their students as well as their mentees about their own passion for learning.

EMBRACING NEW IDEAS

One of the most important ways mentors model being learners is through their openness to new ideas, including the ideas of beginning teachers. When I began my own career as a high school social studies teacher, I was fortunate to join a department where it was clear from the beginning that learning was part of the culture. The teachers whom I had the good fortune to meet that fall talked as much about history, politics, economics, and current affairs as they did about how to teach those subjects. They were hungry, however, for new information about pedagogy as well as content.

At one of my first department meetings, the chair informed us that we had been approved to purchase new American history books for the following year. This began a discussion of what books we should review and the timeline for the selection process. I had just completed my social studies methods course, in which the professor had introduced us to a new inquiry-based approach to teaching history. The "New Social Studies" (1967) had been developed by Edwin Fenton at Carnegie-Mellon University, and I asked if anyone had heard of it. No one had, but they asked me to get more information so that they could order review copies. A month later, after considerable debate, the Fenton text was adopted, and tens of thousands of dollars were spent on the book that the new teacher had recommended. I remember being impressed that these veteran teachers were willing to explore a new approach to teaching American history, especially one recommended by a rookie. More important, I felt validated and accepted as a full member of this new learning community.

Open to New Behaviors

Several years ago, a mentor teacher named Kim shared a story that I have never forgotten. In fact, I have used it often to help make an important point about being open not only to the ideas of beginning teachers, but to their needs as well. Kim was a very successful and highly respected third-grade teacher working in an urban school district where many of the children came from families living in poverty. One year she was assigned to mentor Angie, a 22-year-old, first-year teacher who came from a suburban background.

Angie was very concerned about her students and the challenges that many of them faced in their lives outside of school. According to Kim, Angie had become particularly concerned about David, one of her students who came from a large, single-parent family. Apparently the teacher who had David in her class the previous year shared with Angie some information that she acquired from a social worker who visited David's apartment in the local public housing project. The social worker reported that the mother had a lock on the refrigerator door to prevent the six children, ages 3 to 12, from eating the family's limited food supply while she was at work from 4 P.M. to 12 A.M.

According to Kim, Angie could not seem to let this image of David's home life go. "For three days she kept asking me if I would drive with her to the housing project, because she wanted to see where David lived. This didn't make any sense to me. I tried to explain that there was nothing to be gained by such a trip." Finally, according to Kim, she decided to put her own feelings aside. "It just dawned on me one afternoon that maybe I should just do it. So, we got in my car and went." The two teachers sat in the car outside David's home and talked for a half hour. Kim went on to describe how the trip left her with a deeper understanding of Angie and the challenges she was facing in learning how to teach children who came from a background so different from her own. Finally, Kim said,

"I learned that a beginning teacher's needs are very different from my own and that I need to accept that as okay. What is still interesting to me is that the trip seemed to meet her need."

FORMAL AND INFORMAL TEACHER LEARNING

Beginning teachers tend to enter the profession with relatively narrow conceptions of teacher learning. In contrast, veteran teachers tend to hold broader but frequently unarticulated conceptions of how they have learned how to teach.

In 2000, the National Research Council published a report titled *How People Learn: Brain, Mind, Experience, and School* (Bransford, 2000). The purpose of the publication was to share the latest scientific findings on the process of human learning, and how that process might be facilitated in both formal and informal learning environments. Chapter 8 was simply titled "Teacher Learning." In the opening paragraphs of that chapter, the authors point out that teacher learning is a relatively new area for educational researchers and that the data that exist tend to be in the form of case studies. In the ensuing discussion, the author acknowledges that teacher learning is both informal and formal in nature, and that it occurs in diverse school contexts.

Formal methods of teacher learning are likely the ones most familiar to beginning teachers. Participating in inservice workshops, taking graduate classes, and attending professional conferences all represent formal ways in which teachers learn. Each of these three common approaches to teacher learning provides mentors with opportunities to model a commitment to professional growth by simply sharing their experiences with their beginning teachers. When they do so, they make public their own positive disposition to learning and often find that these reports lead to deeper conversations about the knowledge or skill being acquired, or about their beginning teachers' experiences or interests. High-performance mentors often go one important step further and invite their beginning teachers to participate in such learning experiences with them. They understand that these kinds of shared learning experiences can be outstanding opportunities not only to engage in mutual exploration of professional ideas and experiences, but to build trust and rapport as well.

Informal teacher learning experiences can often be covert in nature, and it is consequently important that mentors help beginning teachers recognize them for the important role they play in learning to teach. Personal experimentation, peer consultation, and collaborative planning and teaching are but three examples of how teachers learn in informal and job-embedded ways. Mentors who openly share how they acquired much of their professional knowledge and skill by running informal experiments in their own classrooms help novices understand that learning to teach is an ongoing process of inquiry, discovery, and application. When mentors talk openly about what they have learned from their colleagues and acknowledge the wisdom of practice that exists in their schools, they create a climate in which their mentees are more likely to recognize peer dialogue and consultation as valued avenues to their own learning. High-performance mentors facilitate this process for novices by making the referrals and connections to those veteran teachers who have the knowledge or skill the beginning teacher needs or wants. Finally, high-performance mentors value team planning and team teaching as particularly potent opportunities for teacher learning. If such opportunities do not occur naturally in the context of their schools, high-performance mentors will often take the initiative to create them.

A FRAMEWORK FOR TEACHER LEARNING

Another way of thinking about teacher learning is to conceptualize it in terms of "what" teachers learn about. One way to do this is also suggested by Bransford (2000), who suggests that teacher learning can be viewed as focusing or "being centered on" three broad and intersecting domains of knowledge. These domains are learner-centered, knowledge-centered, and assessment-centered.

Learner-Centered

The focus of teachers' learning is said to be learner-centered when it deals with how teachers can come to a fuller understanding of the knowledge, skills, attitudes, and beliefs that students bring to the classroom. There are many ways to think about this important area of teacher development, including how teachers employ culturally appropriate practices, uncover students' prior knowledge, and craft learning tasks that constitute respectful work for diverse learners. It is important for mentor teachers to be mindful that some beginning teachers will have a positive disposition toward being learner-centered but may well lack the specific knowledge, skills, and experience to create learner-centered environments for their students. Such beginners will profit most from hearing mentors talk about how they learned specific learner-centered practices. In contrast, others will place far less value on the learner-centered nature of teaching and will require different types of support. The important point to remember is that high-performance mentors share their own experiences in developing their beliefs about learner-centered classrooms, as well as about the specific techniques and strategies they have acquired that help them put those beliefs into action.

Knowledge-Centered

Teachers are knowledge-centered when they seek to learn more about how students develop understanding of subject matter and when they focus on what is known about how students construct new knowledge based on their prior understandings. Most veteran teachers can quickly recall their early experiences with discovering that students held many misconceptions about the subject matter they were teaching, and that such misconceptions were often difficult to overcome. Many beginning teachers, despite strong grade-point averages in their respective teaching fields, are not equipped with a broad range of strategies for helping students develop deep understanding. Still others, to complicate things even more, will bring misconceptions of their own to their first year of teaching. Mentor teachers who describe their personal efforts to learn more about how to help students understand subject matter can open the door to meaningful conversations with beginning teachers that can advance their own learning in this important area of teacher development.

Assessment-Centered

Teachers can be said to be assessment-centered when they seek to learn more about the important roles that formative and summative assessments play in the learning process. Teachers who dedicate themselves to finding better ways to monitor students' understanding and provide timely and appropriate feedback are assessment-centered. Teachers are also assessment-centered when they commit to learning how to diversify their assessment strategies, or provide students with greater opportunities for revising their work to meet established performance standards. Assessment is a critically important but historically undervalued dimension of teaching and learning. Most veteran teachers can easily recount their early experiences in creating student assessments and how their current practices have evolved from those early experiments. Mentors who share their own learning experiences with student assessment and invite mentees to join them in learning more about effective assessment strategies can help their mentees accelerate their efforts to create assessment-centered classrooms.

Figure 7.1 represents the three domains just described as the content or foci of teacher learning in the context of some of the formal and informal ways in which that learning occurs.

The purpose of Figure 7.1 is not only to help mentors reflect on their own learning, but to assist them in thinking about how they might structure the content and methods of learning for beginning teachers as well. Mentors who share the model with their beginning teachers take an important step to helping them develop a framework for thinking about

156

Figure 7.1 Teacher Learning: Methods and Foci

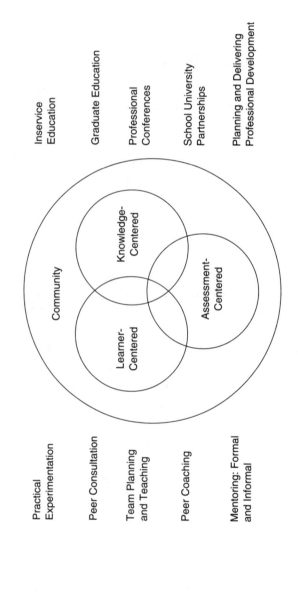

Inservice
Education

Graduate Education

Professional
Conferences

School University
Partnerships

Planning and Delivering
Professional Development

Community

Knowledge-
Centered

Learner-
Centered

Assessment-
Centered

Practical
Experimentation

Peer Consultation

Team Planning
and Teaching

Peer Coaching

Mentoring: Formal
and Informal

their own needs and interests, and how they might be met in both formal and informal learning environments.

LEARNING INDICATORS

The High-Performance Mentoring Framework lists five indicators for *Models a Commitment to Personal and Professional Growth*:

1. Lives the life of learner as well as teacher

2. Engages the mentee as fellow student of teaching and learning

3. Pursues professional growth related to teaching and mentoring

4. Advises the mentee on professional growth opportunities

5. Models fallibility as a quality fundamental to personal and professional growth

Lives the Life of Learner

High-performance mentors have a strong personal disposition toward learning that is apparent to their mentees. Consequently, when they talk about learning to teach as a lifelong process, their words ring true. The fact that the ways in which they learn—and the focus of their learning—vary widely does not matter as much as the fact that they are visible models of learners committed to personal and professional growth. This personal motivation to learn can be a source of inspiration to beginning teachers as they confront the gaps in their own knowledge base. Richard, a first-year science teacher, put it this way: "You learn very quickly that you don't know very much. And it's kind of a slap in the face. You wake up pretty quickly and realize how much learning there is to do." Richard went on to describe how his mentor was able to help him put this reality into perspective. "He told me that it does get easier, but that there are certain parts of the job that are always there, and that learning is one of those parts. I think hearing those words helped me feel more comfortable asking him for help."

Mentors who talk with mentees about their own learning accomplish several things. First, as was the case with Richard, they can help mentees put their own learning in perspective, creating a climate in which beginning teachers are more open to asking for help. Second, by sharing their personal learning goals and interests with their mentees, high-performance mentors increase the likelihood that they might pique the interest of their mentees, creating an opportunity for learning together. Third, when mentors talk explicitly about what they are interested in learning, they help beginning teachers develop a broader and more complex conception of professional practice. Finally, when they share the specific ways in which they are learning, they help their mentees develop a more diversified view of the many and varied ways that teachers can and do learn. Understanding the specific ways that veteran teachers learn through collaboration, self-study, and experimentation, for example, can help beginning teachers think more broadly about their own learning, and how it is not limited to workshops, seminars, or graduate classes.

Students of Teaching and Learning

From my perspective, one of the most powerful conceptions of a mentoring relationship is that of the mentor and mentee as fellow students of teaching and learning. I am so enamored of this conception that I encourage mentors to consider sharing it with their mentees in their initial meetings with them. Many beginning teachers are hesitant, unsure, and at times even anxious about what it will be like to work with a mentor. Sharing the idea that you look forward to learning "with" them can go a long way to allay their fears. Of course, such talk must be followed by congruent action.

Mentors who are committed to the idea of being a co-learner look for ways to place themselves and their beginning teachers in learning contexts that are both formal and informal in nature. For example, they value the opportunity to attend professional conferences, inservice workshops, and other staff development events with their mentees. They know how valuable shared experience can be in stimulating professional dialogue. And after such events, they make every effort to collaborate with their mentees in the application of their new knowledge and skill.

High-performance mentors appreciate the value of job-embedded learning and find creative ways to turn their own schools into learning environments for beginning teachers. For example, they frequently encourage beginning teachers to visit the classrooms of other teachers to observe others in the act of teaching. At a recent workshop, a beginning teacher named Molly gave a strong endorsement to this practice. "It was the best thing my mentor ever did for me, and she did a lot of wonderful things. I learned so much, so quickly. It was amazing." There is also much to be gained when mentor and mentee go together to visit the classroom of another teacher. Once again, the power of shared experience is at work when such a learning strategy is employed. After the observation, mentors have rich opportunities to use the cognitive apprenticeship strategies described in Chapter 6. Other approaches worth considering include reading the same book or journal article, or viewing a professional video of mutual interest. In these and many other ways, mentors invite beginning teachers to become students of the teaching and learning process in the way that Palmer (1998) described it when he wrote the following:

When I imagine the community of truth gathered around some great thing—from DNA to *The Heart of Darkness* to the French Revolution—I wonder: Could teachers gather around the great thing called "teaching and learning" and explore its mysteries with the same respect we accord any subject worth knowing? (p. 141)

Pursues Professional Growth

Richard, the first-year science teacher I mentioned earlier, described his initial shock when his mentor, a veteran science teacher, informed him that after 16 years he is still searching for new ways to teach. "He told me that the planning and preparation parts of the job are always there and that he feels an obligation to his students to keep informed about the latest scientific discoveries in his field." Responding to my inquiry about mentors as models of continuous learners, a beginning teacher named Diane shared her surprise when she learned that her mentor was attending mentor training. "I had no idea that she was going to evening workshops until the day she showed me a framework for thinking about the stages of a teaching career. I was impressed that she seemed really interested in what she was learning, and that she was that dedicated to the job of being my mentor."

Personal and Professional Advisor

Today's beginning teachers face professional development challenges that many veteran teachers did not experience throughout their careers. New state mandates aimed at improving the quality of the teaching force have created new and different requirements for professional development. Although these new standards for teacher quality vary from state to state, they often include some form of entry-year assessment, the preparation of individualized professional development plans, as well as requirements for earning a master's degree or its equivalent within so many years.

Another way in which mentors can model a disposition to learning is by using such beginning teacher requirements as the impetus for their own learning. Mentors who take a positive interest in the learning challenges facing beginning teachers can be a major source of support. Those who dismiss or condemn the new requirements and refuse to learn about what is being asked of their mentees typically fail at two levels. First, because they don't understand the entry-year assessment process, for example, they cannot help their mentee prepare. Second, because they cannot help them prepare for the assessment, whatever form it takes, they communicate a lack of caring for the mentee facing a significant and often anxiety-provoking event.

Models Fallibility

Becoming a successful classroom teacher, or a successful mentor, requires a certain willingness to take reasonable risks. Of course, to take a risk is to open oneself up to the mistakes and failures that are an inevitable part of the learning process. High-performance mentors understand the importance of risk taking and the role it plays in their own professional development, but they also understand the role of fallibility as well. Teachers who try to project an infallible attitude in their classroom do a disservice to their students, sending them the message that there is no room for failure in their own work. Such a classroom climate is counterproductive, suggests Haberman (1995), because it fails to honor the truth that mistakes are critical to the learning process. Good mentors share their historic and current mistakes and misjudgments with their mentees, recognizing that doing so helps beginning teachers realize that "being perfect" is not a reasonable goal in an enterprise as complex as teaching.

QUESTIONS FOR REFLECTION ON LEARNING

- In what specific ways do you live the life of learner as well as teacher?
- Have you found the methods to authentically share those ways with your beginning teacher?
- Are you open to the ideas of beginning teachers?
- Do you recognize the needs or interests of beginning teachers as possible opportunities for your own learning?
- Do you share with beginning teachers your own motivation to learn?

- Have you found ways to place yourself in situations where you and your beginning teacher can function as co-learners?
- Have you shared with your beginning teacher the many and varied ways that you have learned about teaching, both formally and informally?
- Are you willing to model fallibility by describing the mistakes you made in the process of learning to teach?
- Do you think of mentoring as both a "teaching" and "learning" experience?

8

Inspiring

A teacher who is attempting to teach without inspiring the pupil with a desire to learn is hammering on cold iron.

—Horace Mann

The glory of friendship is not the outstretched hand, nor the kindly smile . . . it's the spiritual inspiration that comes to one when he discovers that someone else believes in him.

—Ralph Waldo Emerson

In everyone's life, at some time, our inner fire goes out. It is then burst into flame by an encounter with another human being.

—Albert Schweitzer

I remember an occasion from my early years in higher education, when an administrator used the term "inspirational puffball" to describe the kind of leader he was not interested in hiring for an important leadership position in the university. The upshot of the remark was that he was looking for someone with solid academic credentials. I was intrigued by that image and have tried to develop an opposing one that would describe someone with great intelligence, but no capacity to inspire. I am not sure I am happy with it, but perhaps "intellectual boulder" gets close. The point of this exercise in metaphor is to remind us that beginning teachers are not likely to be inspired by mentors who are little more than motivational coaches trying to inspire with sentimental words and poignant stories. In similar fashion, mentees are not likely to be inspired by mentors who believe that all things educational are intellectual, and that inspiring new teachers comes from mentors brandishing their own knowledge.

Personal Reflections on Inspiration

For more than 25 years, I spent each summer guiding high school students on wilderness canoe trips into Canada's Quetico Provincial Park, a vast and watery wilderness of lakes and streams just north of the Minnesota border. For most of those years, I was a high school teacher, and many of the students had been in my classes the previous school year. Thinking back, I clearly remember telling friends and family members that I felt I did some of my best teaching on those summer trips.

One of the reasons I felt good about my teaching in that environment was that I was involved in fully sharing the experience with the students. We were on the same journey, facing the same challenges every day. Every swampy portage they encountered, I mucked through as well. Every head wind they battled made my own arms ache. Equally important, we marveled at the same displays of the northern lights. We sat in silence around the same dying campfires and listened together to the calls of the loons. Perhaps equally important, we found humor in our own and each other's mistakes and idiosyncratic behaviors. The things we laughed at buoyed our spirits. Each evening, the struggles of the day mellowed as camp was set and the bantering began. New words emerged in an attempt to describe the subtleties of our experience. Out of the context of our group, those words had no meaning, but whispered in the woods they could trigger a smile or a belly laugh. Early in the trip, students were often overwhelmed by some of the things they were asked to do. They no doubt were dismayed, for example, when awakened at dawn to learn that we would travel in the rain because the waters were calm. At the end of the trip, while sitting on the porch of the lodge watching the rain on the lake, a sophomore might simply say "good travel day" and immediately be understood.

Today, I have a deeper understanding that I was part of a powerful learning experience in which I played the role of mentor as well as guide. Now I believe that it had mostly to do with the sense that I was introducing young people to a new world, a world that had come to mean so much in my own life. Almost all the students who signed up for the trips had very little, if any, prior camping experience. Some of them had been Boy Scouts or Girl Scouts, whereas others had gone camping on rare occasions with their parents. Few of them had any real idea of the physical and emotional challenges they would face, or the pristine beauty they would experience. They signed up, if you will, as enthusiastic beginners with great visions of what the trip would be. By the end of the first day of paddling and portaging, most of those visions had been seriously compromised and many students were full of doubt as to whether they would survive the next 7 days.

It was fascinating to watch how different individuals reacted to the demands they were facing. It did not take me very long to recognize that gender, physical size, or athletic prowess were poor predictors of performance in this environment. My partner Mack, a fellow teacher, and I had a policy with regard to whom we were willing to accept. Basically, the policy was that we would take anyone who could get a physician's approval to participate. Consequently, we often took students whom fellow teachers thought we were "crazy" for including. One year we would be crazy because a student had a reputation for being a discipline problem. The next year we might be crazy because a student was too heavy, or too thin. In almost every case—and there were many—the trip was especially memorable because "that student" was part of the experience.

One of the most gratifying things over the years has been watching the effects that those trips had on many of the young people. They signed up with high confidence and low competence, but returned to base camp with new confidence anchored in experience, and new skills acquired in practice on the trail. They were now prepared to return without our guidance, and yet many chose to return with us to have the same experience throughout their high school years.

Today, many of those same students guide their friends, spouses, and children on the same lakes and streams they paddled in their youth. There is a great sense of personal meaningfulness in knowing that you have impacted a person's life in such a way. I prefer personal meaningfulness over "pride" because I know that what inspired them to return was a constellation of experiences that far transcended my role as their guide. I like to think that I was in that constellation and that through my presence, encouragement, and companionship, the experience was somehow enriched. The most powerful force that brings them back, I believe, is a yearning to once again find themselves responsible for themselves, in a wilderness world of sights, sounds, and smells that have worked their way into the very fabric of their being. They are, I believe, inspired to return.

Mentoring a new teacher can be a wonderfully adventurous experience when two persons, one a veteran and one a beginner, join together for the adventure that is the school year. Each brings his or her own knowledge, skills, and dispositions to begin the journey. When the relationship works, the beginning teacher is welcomed to a new world, guided through the many challenges, and leaves inspired to return. The day before I began writing this chapter, I had an experience that reinforced these insights.

It was mid-June. Earlier in the school year, I had facilitated a workshop designed to support teachers in designing problem-based learning experiences that would require them to develop knowledge and skill in things such as backward design, differentiated instruction, cooperative learning, and technology integration. Two of the participants were a mentor-mentee team. Janet and Amy were middle school language arts teachers. In January, I had observed them as they worked together to plan a unit that would engage their students in confronting contemporary issues of social justice by studying the Civil Rights Movement of the 1960s. The mentor was in her 27th year of teaching. The beginning teacher was a 27-year-old who had come to teaching after 4 years of working for a corporate public relations firm. It had been fun to watch the two of them as they engaged in the various workshop activities and shared the experience of being students.

My recent opportunity to see them again occurred when they returned for a summer follow-up session. They sat side by side at the conference table as they reported on their new unit and shared with other teachers what had worked well, what they needed to change, and most important, how students had responded to the experience. It was clear that their relationship was one of friendship and mutual respect. The beginning teacher did most of the reporting, and it was apparent from her nonverbal messages that the mentor was pleased to have her do so. Several times throughout the report, they shared eye contact that was very easy to read. Amy's glance, which seemed to say "How am I doing?" was returned by one from Janet that clearly said: "Keep going. You're doing great."

After describing the various learning activities they had crafted around a multiple intelligence framework, I interrupted to share how impressed I was with their work. At that point, Janet quickly spoke. "Amy is responsible for that part. She is so creative when it comes to thinking about differentiation. I am learning so much from her. In fact, I am trying to convince her to do a workshop for our staff." Their unit had gone better than expected, with many of their initial fears unrealized. However, what was clear to me as Amy and Janet reported was that they were keenly aware that their report could only touch the surface of their shared experience.

INSPIRATION INDICATORS

The High-Performance Mentoring Framework lists five indicators for *Inspires Hope and Optimism for the Future.* Clearly, inspiration is a complex and personal phenomenon that in many ways defies easy explanation. Nonetheless, the following five behaviors are a good place to start one's thinking about inspiring beginning teachers. Specifically, the high-performance mentor:

1. Encourages and praises the mentee

2. Holds and communicates high expectations for the mentee

3. Projects a positive disposition toward the teaching profession

4. Avoids criticism of students, parents, and colleagues

5. Models personal and professional self-efficacy

Encourages and Praises the Mentee

Some teachers are not at ease encouraging or praising other teachers. I share this observation in the hope that you might reflect on your own comfort level in this area. Many beginning teachers are hungry for both encouragement and praise as they work through the survival concerns that are a predictable part of the first-year experience. In interviewing beginning teachers, I often hear statements such as, "I think I am doing an okay job, but nobody ever tells me that I am." Or, "Driving home at night, I find myself wondering if I am doing anything right."

High-performance mentors look for opportunities to encourage beginning teachers when they are endeavoring to complete a challenging task or develop a new skill. Mentors like Janet, for example, understand that the same rules of praise that work in their classrooms apply to beginning teachers as well. They know that specific praise is preferable to generalized praise in at least two important ways. First, specific praise automatically communicates interest, attention, and authenticity. Second, it reinforces important behaviors, thought patterns, or dispositions that the mentor would like to see the novice continue.

Holds and Communicates High Expectations

One of the most powerful messages a mentor teacher can send a novice teacher is that he or she believes the beginner is capable of doing great things. When Janet, in front of her colleagues, disclosed that she was trying to convince Amy to offer a workshop, it was clear that she understood the power of holding and communicating high expectations.

Projects a Positive Disposition

Whether wilderness camping or teaching, novices and veterans alike are going to experience some days that are more challenging, more frustrating than others. One thing that outdoor adventuring and classroom teaching have in common is that both are full of surprises, some good and some bad. The portage trail that peters out in a dead-end swamp is as disheartening as the lesson plan that dries up in the face of student apathy. The sight of the moose cow and calf caught crossing the river is as thrilling as the unexpected performance of a reluctant learner. Just as good guides must project a positive demeanor in the face of adversity, good mentors must maintain a positive disposition toward their work. This does not mean that they project joy when disappointment is the reality, or cheerfulness when disenchantment is in the air. What it does mean is that they acknowledge the lows in the context of the highs while staying the course.

Avoids Criticism

When things go bad on the wilderness trail, novices can quickly become critical and look for someone to blame for the problems they are encountering. Sometimes a fellow camper becomes the object of criticism, whereas at other times it is the guide. This is as dangerous and debilitating in the schoolhouse as it is in the backcountry. Good mentors, like good guides, are vigilant in their attention to this enemy, always mindful that they must project a demeanor that rises above these efforts to divert responsibility to others. As I remind mentors-in-training, you must be prepared to take the high trail when others are stirring up the muck in the swamp of gossip, innuendo, and misplaced blame.

Models Personal and Professional Self-Efficacy

The word *inspire* finds its root in the Latin word *inspirare*, which means to breathe, or to breathe into. High-performance mentors can inspire or breathe new life into beginning teachers in many ways. My own sense is that beginning teachers are most likely to be inspired by interacting with mentors who are authentic, self-actualizing persons who are living the life they hope to live. Such mentors communicate hope and optimism for the future. They inspire beginning teachers to continue forward in the face of so many forces that work to push them back and steal their spirit and resolve. In the end, I believe that it takes all five of the previously examined qualities of the high-performance mentor to be an inspirational force in the life of a beginning teacher. Committing, accepting, communicating, coaching, and learning all have a part to play in building the kind of relationship that can inspire a beginning teacher to fully embrace the teaching life.

QUESTIONS FOR REFLECTION ON INSPIRING

- Do you believe that mentor teachers have the capacity to be a source of inspiration for beginning teachers?
- Have you identified those persons who have been a source of inspiration in your own life?

- Have you reflected on what specific aspects of their personhood were inspirational?
- Do you look for opportunities to encourage or praise beginning teachers for specific endeavors or accomplishments?
- Do you endeavor to maintain a positive disposition toward your work despite the challenges you encounter and the setbacks you suffer?
- Do you avoid placing blame on others and model personal efficacy in seeking solutions to the problems you confront?
- Does your beginning teacher feel that you are on the same great adventure?
- Do you believe your beginning teacher looks to you for leadership and support when they encounter frustration or loss of resolve?

Bibliography

Bey, T. M., & Holmes, C. T. (Eds.). (1992). *Mentoring: Contemporary principles and issues.* Reston, VA: Association of Teacher Educators.

Blanchard, K. (Speaker). (1993). *Personal excellence: Where achievement and fulfillment meet* (Cassette Recording Side 7). Chicago: Nightingale-Conant.

Brammer, L. M. (1993). *The helping relationship: Process and skills* (5th ed.). New York: HarperCollins.

Bransford, J. D. (2000). *How people learn: Brain, mind, experience, and school.* Washington, DC: National Academy Press.

Brophy, J., & Good, T. (1991). *Looking in classrooms* (5th ed.). New York: HarperCollins.

Clawson, J. (1980). Mentoring and managerial careers. In C. B. Derr (Ed.), *Work, family, and the career* (pp. 144–165). New York: Praeger.

Collins, A., Brown, J. S., & Newman, S. E. (1990). Cognitive apprenticeship: Teaching the craft of reading, writing, and mathematics. In L. B. Resnick (Ed.), *Knowing, learning, and instruction: Essays in honor of Robert Glaser.* Hillsdale, NJ: Erlbaum.

Combs, A. W., Blume, R. A., Newman, A. J., & Wass, H. L. (1974). *The professional education of teachers: A humanistic approach to teacher preparation* (2nd ed.). Boston: Allyn & Bacon.

Costa, A., & Garmston, R. (1994). *Cognitive coaching: A foundation for renaissance schools.* Norwood, MA: Christopher-Gordon.

Csikszentmihalyi, M. (1977). *Beyond boredom and anxiety.* San Francisco: Jossey-Bass.

Csikszentmihalyi, M. (1997). *Finding flow: The psychology of engagement with everyday life.* New York: HarperCollins.

Danielson, C. (1996). *Enhancing professional practice: A framework for teaching.* Alexandria, VA: Association for Supervision and Curriculum Development.

DePree, M. (1989). *Leadership is an art.* New York: Doubleday.

Fenton, E. (1967). *The new social studies.* New York: Holt, Rinehart and Winston.

Fuller, F. F. (1969). Concerns of teachers: A developmental conceptualization. *American Education Research Journal, 6,* 207–226.

Gazda, G. M., Asbury, F., Balzer, F. J., Childers, W. C., & Walters, R. P. (1991). *Human relations development: A manual for educators* (4th ed.). Boston: Allyn & Bacon.

Glickman, C. D. (1985). *Supervision of instruction: A developmental approach.* Boston: Allyn & Bacon.

Glickman, C. D. (2002). *Leadership for learning: How to help teachers succeed.* Alexandria, VA: Association for Supervision and Curriculum Development.

Goldhammer, R. (1969). *Clinical supervision: Special methods for the supervision of teachers.* New York: Holt, Rinehart, and Winston.

Good, T. L., & Brophy, J. E. (2000). *Looking in classrooms* (8th ed.). White Plains, NY: Longman.

Gordon, S. P. (1990). *Assisting the entry-year teacher: A leadership resource.* Columbus: Ohio Department of Education.

Haberman, M. (1995). *Star teachers of children in poverty.* West Lafayette, IN: Kappa Delta Pi.

Head, F. A., Reiman, A. J., & Thies-Sprinthall, L. (1992). The reality of mentoring: Complexity in its process and function. In T. M. Bey & C. T. Holmes (Eds.), *Mentoring: Contemporary principles and issues* (pp. 5–24). Reston, VA: Association of Teacher Educators.

Hersey, P., & Blanchard, K. (1974). So you want to know your leadership style? *Training and Development Journal, 28*(2), 1–15.

Huling-Ausin, L. (1992). Introduction. In T. M. Bey & C. T. Holmes (Eds.), *Mentoring: Contemporary principles and issues* (pp. 1–4). Reston, VA: Association of Teacher Educators.

Knowles, M. S. (1975). *Self-directed learning: A guide for learners and teachers.* Chicago: Association Press.

Knowles, M. S. (1978). *The adult learner: A neglected species.* Houston, TX: Gulf.

Krupp, J. A. (1982). *The adult learner: A unique entity.* Manchester, CT: Adult Development and Learning.

Lacey, C. (1977). *The socialization of teachers.* London: Methuen.

Maslow, A. H. (1943). A theory of human motivation. *Psychological Review, 50,* 370–396.

Palmer, P. J. (1998). *The courage to teach: Exploring the inner landscape of a teacher's life.* San Francisco: Jossey-Bass.

Pinár, W. F. (1989). A reconceptualization of teacher education. *Journal of Teacher Education, 40*(1), 9–12.

Rogers, C. (1958). The characteristics of a helping profession. *Personnel and Guidance Journal, 37,* 6–16.

Rogers, C. R. (1961). *On becoming a person.* Boston: Houghton Mifflin.

Rowley, J. (1999). The good mentor. *Educational Leadership, 56*(8), 20–22.

Rowley, J. B. (2005). Teacher mentoring and induction: The state of the art and beyond. In H. Portner (Ed.), *Mentor teachers as instructional coaches* (pp. 109–127). Thousand Oaks, CA: Corwin Press.

Rowley, J. B., & Hart, P. M. (2000). *High-performance mentoring: A multimedia program for training mentor teachers.* Thousand Oaks, CA: Corwin Press.

Schön, D. (1987). *Educating the reflective practitioner.* San Francisco: Jossey-Bass.

Veenman, S. (1984). Perceived problems of beginning teachers. *Review of Educational Research, 54*(2), 143–178.

Weigel, V. B. (2002). *Deep learning for a digital age: Technology's untapped potential to enrich higher education.* San Francisco: Jossey-Bass.

Wolfe, D. M. (1992). Designing training and selecting incentives for mentor programs. In T. M. Bey & C. T. Holmes (Eds.), *Mentoring: Contemporary principles and issues* (pp. 103–110). Reston, VA: Association of Teacher Educators.

Zeichner, K., & Gore, J. (1990). Teacher socialization. In W. R. Houston (Ed.), *Handbook of research on teacher education* (pp. 311–328). New York: Macmillan.

Index

**CORWIN
PRESS**

The Corwin Press logo—a raven striding across an open book—represents the union of courage and learning. Corwin Press is committed to improving education for all learners by publishing books and other professional development resources for those serving the field of PreK–12 education. By providing practical, hands-on materials, Corwin Press continues to carry out the promise of its motto: **"Helping Educators Do Their Work Better."**